GESTALT THERAPY

Other books by the same author

- **Jeunesse et difficultés d'adaptation** in *Une nouvelle jeunesse française* (editor: JOUSSELIN J.). Privat, Toulouse, 1966.
- **La psychopédagogie, mal indispensable ou science qui se cherche** in *L'équipe de psychiatrie et son psychiatre*. Privat, 1966.
- **La profession d'Éducateur spécialisé et ses perspectives** in *Sciences de l'homme et professions sociales* (editor: CRAPUCHET S.). Toulouse, Privat, 1974.
- *Les interventions éducatives (in Persian)*. Éditions universitaires, Téhéran, 1976. *160 p.*
- *Nouvelles lettres persanes: Journal d'un Français à Téhéran (1974–1980)* Anthropos, Paris, 1981. *255 p. (Grand prix international du reportage)*
- **La Gestalt-thérapie et quelques autres approches humanistes, dans la pratique hospitalière**, in *Former à l'Hôpital* (editor: HONORÉ B.). Privat, Toulouse, 1983.
- **La Gestalt, une troisième voie? Développement personnel et sexualité** in *Le Développement personnel et les Travailleurs sociaux* (editors: VANOYE et GINGER), ESF, Paris, 1985.
- *La Gestalt, une thérapie du contact (translated into 6 languages). (with Anne GINGER)*, Hommes et Gr, Paris, 1987 (7e ed: 2003). *550 p.*
- *La Gestalt: l'art du contact (translated into 11 languages)*. Paris, 1995. Guide de poche Marabout n° 3554. (19th ed.: 2007). *290 p.*
- *Lexique international de Gestalt-thérapie (in eight languages)* FORGE, Paris, 1995. *176 p.*
- **Foreword** of *Manuel de Gestalt-thérapie* de Fritz PERLS, ESF, Paris, 2003, 128 p.; 2nd edition: 2005.
- **La Gestalt-thérapie aujourd'hui**, in *A quel psy se vouer?*, editor: ELKAÏM M., Le Seuil, Paris, 2003.
- **Foreword** of *Pourquoi la Psychothérapie? Fondements, méthodes, applications*, editor: NGUYEN T., Dunod, Paris, 2005.
- **Foreword** of *La Gestalt-thérapie, un processus créatif*, ZINKER J., Dunod, Paris, 2006.
- *Psychothérapie: 100 réponses pour en finir avec les idées reçues*. Dunod, Paris, 2006, *290 p.*
- *Être psychothérapeute*, editors: GINGER S., MARC E., TARPINIAN A., Dunod, Paris, 2006, *270 p.*
- **Un regard gestaltiste sur la supervision** in *La supervision en psychanalyse et en psychothérapie*, editors: DELOURME A., MARC E., Dunod, Paris, 2006.

... and 150 articles published in 23 different countries.

GESTALT THERAPY

The Art of Contact

Serge Ginger

Translated by
Sarah Spargo & Sally Reeder Cojean

Routledge
Taylor & Francis Group

LONDON AND NEW YORK

First published 2007 by Karnac Books Ltd

Published 2018 by Routledge
2 Park Square, Milton Park, Abingdon, Oxon OX14 4RN
711 Third Avenue, New York, NY 10017, USA

Routledge is an imprint of the Taylor & Francis Group, an informa business

French original edition:
La Gestalt: l'art du contact
Collection: Guides de poche *Psychologie*, **n° 3554**

1st edition:	© 1995. Marabout, Bruxelles.
4th edition:	© 2000. Marabout/Hachette, Paris.
9th edition:	© 2007. Marabout/Hachette, Paris.

Translated into:

- Spanish
- Italian
- Russian
- Polish
- Romanian
- Ukrainian
- Latvian
- Portuguese
- Japanese
- Macedonian
- English

British Library Cataloguing in Publication Data

A C.I.P for this book is available from the British Library

ISBN 9781855755710 (pbk)

Edited, designed, and produced by
Florence Production Ltd, Stoodleigh, Devon
www.florenceproduction.co.uk

CONTENTS

ABOUT THE AUTHOR

Serge Ginger has been one of the pioneers of Gestalt Therapy in France, since 1970. With his wife, Anne Ginger, he founded the *Paris School of Gestalt* (*École Parisienne de Gestalt*, EPG), in 1980- which is actually one of the leading Gestalt Training institutes in Europe.

He is a clinical Psychologist, Psychoanalyst, Psychodramatist and Gestalt Therapist and teaches Gestalt in France and throughout the world (France, Belgium, Switzerland, Italy, Russia, Romania, Poland, Latvia, Brazil, Mexico, Norway, USA, and Japan).

He is currently the President of the *International Federation of Gestalt Training Organizations* (FORGE), Secretary General of the French *National Umbrella for Psychotherapy* (*Fédération Française de Psychothérapie et Psychanalyse*, FF2P) and the Registrar of the *European Association for Psychotherapy* (EAP).

FOREWORD
Ken Evans

Over the next two pages I trust I will inspire you to read and enjoy this creative and original book by Serge Ginger, cofounder with his wife, Anne, of the Paris School of Gestalt (Ecole Parisienne de Gestalt) in 1980.

Some years ago, a wise woman said to me, "When you meet a Gestalt Therapist, you meet a real person." (Marianne Fry, personal communication) A Gestalt therapist brings their authentic presence to the therapeutic meeting and they will work alongside you, without negative judgement, supporting and encouraging you to discover who you really are and who you may become.

In this book, you will encounter not only fine words, ideas and theories. More importantly, you will meet Serge Ginger – the man. He has written this book in such a way that his presence and authenticity, expressed from his heart as well as his head, light up the pages. So let me describe to you something of the qualities of the person you will meet as you continue to read this book.

I first met Serge Ginger when I was President of the European Association for Psychotherapy (EAP) in the mid-1990's. To be honest, I found him somewhat intimidating at first! Who was this articulate and intelligent French man who seemed to appear from nowhere at every committee meeting, encouraging and motivating his colleagues to greater professionalism and ethical endeavor? And where did he get his seemingly inexhaustible supply of energy, that left much younger colleagues amazed?

With the creation of the European Certificate for Psychotherapy in 1997, it was no surprise that his colleagues and peers in the EAP entrusted him with the important task of evaluating and monitoring applications for certification across 26 (now 41) European nations. We all felt confident that this was the right person for the task. It was not simply his impressive intellect and energy, but also his ability to confront the comfortable and pompous often with a mischievous grin. Both philosophical and pragmatic, here was a man capable of promoting the credibility of the psychotherapy profession by championing fairness and justice, irrespective of reputation, position or nationality.

Through the pages of this book, *Gestalt Therapy – The Art of Contact*, you will be able to meet Serge Ginger, intelligent, articulate, energetic, supportive, challenging and provocative. If you are a member of the public interested in finding out more about Psychotherapy, then this book will prove accessible and informative. If you are a potential trainee or client, this book will prove a useful preparation, possibly even a trigger to explore further and more deeply the richness and color of the Gestalt approach.

What I believe you will also discern in this book is the quality of compassion that drives, perhaps compels, Serge Ginger to continue to write, teach and practice as a Gestalt therapist at the age of 79. Finally, through this book, Serge Ginger communicates that he is genuinely interested in you, the reader. Beyond all the exciting and revolutionary ideas contained here, what drives him is his desire that you proceed to find ways to experience a deeper meaning and purpose in life, and to defy the isolation, loneliness and anonymity that increasingly permeates the modern world.

I trust that this book will be a door to a deeper exploration of your self such that you may:

Live life fully
Love generously
and
Become all that you can be.

Ken Evans
President, European Association for Gestalt Therapy
Past President EAP
Normandy, France
April 2007

INTRODUCTION

Urgently needed: more human contact!

One of the main features of our time is the massive development of "real-time" communications: newspapers, radio, telephone, television, fax, internet, etc. have become more and more widespread. We all witness the humanitarian crisis in Kosovo, the rocket landing in Siberia, the rugby match in Australia, the terrorist attack of September 11th . . .

The whole world is right there in our living room, *whether we like it . . . or not.*

The character of *simple human contact* is denatured by such media technology: we meet each other less often by choice, contact is often by chance, and we "zap" from one thing to the another, as the fancy takes us.

Paradoxically, now that the world has invaded our homes (not just television and internet, but the mobile telephone—which interrupts any conversation without warning), we feel more isolated than ever before. *Depression*, the "illness of the century", affects almost 40% of the population, at one moment or another. There are *millions* of people in the world taking *Prozac!*

What can be done to ward off the loneliness and anonymity that result from our *"depersonalizing"* technology? How can we develop and share *human warmth* through authentic encounters? How can we encourage creativity, the *right to be different*, and at the same time let each person lead his life as it suits them[1] and be recognized for who they are? How can we help vulnerable people clearly see closed *sects* for what they really are, a misleading *illusion* of safety?

Gestalt Therapy, and other branches of *Humanistic Psychology*, developed in an attempt to respond to these challenges, amongst others.

The Gestalt revolution

In this book we will see that Gestalt Therapy proposes a *new, and even revolutionary way of life*. We will show why this method, originally European, underwent such successful development in the United States of America and then throughout Europe, Russia and even Japan. Gestalt is now present in the medical and social fields, and is penetrating the private sector.

Cartesian thought maintains that any phenomenon or behavior must be *understood* before it can be changed, that the *past cause* must be found (by objective analysis) before the problem can be solved. But now, developments in physics and *Postmodern Paradigm* seem to reflect Gestalt thought: truly objective observation is impossible (the act of observation *alters* the observed physical object, just as the mere presence of an observer changes the behavior of an observed subject). *Chaos theory* mocks us with uncertainty: could it be true that most "causes" are actually in our future? Everything we know has become uncertain . . . and yet perhaps we could feel it coming with our *right brain*, the intuitive side (as opposed to the left-sided rational brain), which chooses tonight's film, or our life partner!

Why are you reading these lines, in this book? What is the "cause"? Maybe it's the next obvious step in a logical sequence of events: it was recommended by a friend, so you bought it? Here we continue in a traditional vein, identifying the *past cause* of the present situation . . . But maybe you came across the book "by chance", just because you saw it on the shelf? The cause is thus *present*. Maybe you *feel* it could be interesting, even useful in your daily life, both personal and professional? So you look through it for new ideas, to learn and understand: the reason for your interest is thus in the *future*, a discovery-in-waiting. The question is no longer "why" are you reading, but "what for": traditional *causalism* (so dear to science and psychoanalysis) gives way to finalism (or *purposefulness*, as exemplified by art and Gestalt). Another example: why did I go to bed early last night? I was certainly tired (past cause), but in fact I wanted to be well-rested for the seminar *today* (future cause).

Just like modern cars, we function with "front-wheel drive" more often than with rear-wheel drive. We are "pulled along" by our projects, just as we are "pushed forward" by our past. We function in four-wheel drive mode! Gestalt Therapy is complementary to psychoanalytical thought (long-term archeological excavation to reveal the *past*, which partly conditions us): Gestalt concentrates on *the present and the future*. In this way we can become aware of the freedom to build anew. As Lao-Tseu said (Chinese philosopher who founded Taoism, around 500 BC), a lantern at the *back* of the car sheds little light on the road ahead!

Many of our habits, that have become certainties, deserve to be examined. Let us savor the plethora of paradoxes! Contrary to popular thought, we will see that:

- We are equally influenced by past and future,
- Synthesis often precedes analysis,
- The surface reveals as much as the hidden depths,
- Theories are but temporary hypotheses,
- Aggression is a necessary "life drive",
- Symptom amplification can help healing,
- Pleasure is more effective than effort,
- Excessive emotional restraint can lead to cancer,
- Adaptation can impoverish,
- Content may be less important than context: "how" is more significant than "why".

These things and many others, which punctuate this book, are part of what we could call the "**Gestalt Revolution**".

Gestalt can help us to renew our values and value systems, freely and responsibly.

This book

This book is not a Gestalt course. It does not aim to *teach* something— which must be *experienced*: is it possible to appreciate a symphony or a painting by reading about it, or to learn to swim without getting wet?

For those of you who already have some experience of Gestalt, and who want to know more, there is another book in French by the same author which is more detailed and yet remains accessible: *La Gestalt, une thérapie du contact*, Paris, 1987 (*8th edition: 2005*). This is a reference book especially for trainees and therapists—already published in 6 languages.

This English translation is meant to be an *introduction* to Gestalt, for the general public, for those who want to live with their times, who want a *new understanding* of what happens around us and with us, as a new century begins—a century of communication, of cultural exchange, of *contact*. It is not scientifically *exhaustive*, but offers *food for thought*. We also include items of cultural and practical interest, concerning the brain, dreams, sexuality, etc.

Reading the chapters in order is suggested, but each may be read independently, or in order of interest (*disorder* which is characteristic of individual initiative). If you are eager to understand a particular concept, please refer to the *glossary* or the *index*.

Finally, the last chapter summarizes *Twenty fundamental Concepts in Gestalt Therapy*.

Gestalt Therapy is still growing all over the world: there are now specialized training institutes in 50 countries of all continents, and more than 20 Journals. It became one of the most wide-spread psychotherapies after psychoanalysis and cognitive-behavior therapies.

This introductory book has already been translated into Spanish, Italian, Russian, Polish, Ukrainian, Romanian, Latvian and Japanese.

I wish you enjoyable reading! I always enjoy hearing my readers' reactions. So feel free to contact me:

Serge Ginger
Paris, 2007
ginger@noos.fr

Note

1. *Translator's note:* for simplicity, we have kept the French masculine form to include both genders.

CHAPTER ONE

What is Gestalt?

Gestalt Theory

OK, so why do we use this unusual word **Gestalt**, and what exactly does it mean?

In fact, *Gestalt* is a German word. That's why it is spelt with a capital G, except when used as an adjective. Gestalt is sometimes translated as "shape, form or figure" (as in "*Gestalt Theory*" = "theory of shape or form"), but the real meaning of the word is much richer and more complex, and is impossible to translate. That is why we use the German word in English, Russian, French and even Japanese!

The verb *gestalten* means "to give shape or significant structure to". The result, the *Gestalt*, is a complete shape or figure, which has *structure* and *meaning*. For example, a *table* may take on a different meaning, if it is used for work (covered with books) or for dining (set with tablecloth, plates and cutlery): its overall *Gestalt* has changed.

Since the very beginning of our life, the first important "shape" or "figure" that we recognize is a *Gestalt*: our mother's face. The newborn does not distinguish the details, but the form as a whole is "significant" for him.

The way we see things follows certain rules: a global appreciation (such as a human face) cannot be reduced to the sensory appreciation of each component; similarly, water is not just oxygen and hydrogen, neither is a symphony a simple string of notes. In each of these examples, *the whole is different from the sum of its parts.*

1

At the same time, *a part within a whole is different from the part on its own, or the same part within another whole*—the part's identity depends upon its position and function relative to the whole. Thus, a shout at a ball game is not the same as a shout in a deserted street; singing naked in the shower is quite different to singing naked in Times Square!

In order to understand a particular behavior or situation, it is not enough to *analyze* it. A *synthetic* point of view is most important, to appreciate the situation in the larger *overall context*. Rather than paying attention only to details, we can step back and see the "big picture": the "context" is often more important than the "text". To appreciate a political event in another country, it is not enough to send a foreign correspondent; it is more important to have a global, *synthetic* appreciation of the international economy and an understanding of what is at stake.

Gestalt Therapy

Having touched on some of the general principles of Gestalt *Theory*, let us turn to what this book is really about: the applications in Gestalt *Therapy* (GT). To avoid confusion, I could systematically use the word "therapy", but I will deliberately refrain from doing so, as "therapy" is often interpreted as "treatment of *illness*", in spite of the statement from the WHO (the *World Health Organization*) saying that:

> "Health is *not* the absence of illness or of infirmity, but is a state of complete physical, mental and social well-being."

In such a global, "holistic" (from the Greek, "holos", whole) point of view, Gestalt therapy aims for the development and maintenance of such a harmonious state and not for a "cure". Cure refers implicitly to a state of "normality", which is the opposite of the Gestalt approach. In Gestalt, the *right to be different* is highly valued, as is the uniqueness of each person.

This notion of *therapy* is similar to that of *personal development*, the growth of human potential. It is quite different from normalizing influences, based on health and social adaptation. The very first Greek "therapists" were not caretakers, they were *slaves*, whose job was looking after statues of gods; subsequently, there was a Jewish sect of monks, called "therapists", who analyzed sacred texts. Both of these roles involved strengthening the links between gods and men or between Heaven and Earth, mind and matter, between the Word and the flesh. To begin with, therapy sought *psychosomatic harmony* and not medical care. This is the sense that has most meaning in the "new humanistic therapies", which include Gestalt.

Thus, for Goldstein (New York, 1934), one of Perls' (the founder of Gestalt) mentors,

> *"Normal must be defined, not by adaptation, but on the contrary, by the ability to invent new norms."*

Gestalt Therapy: who is it for?

Gestalt Therapy is used in a variety of situations, with multiple aims:

- *Individual* psychotherapy (the client with the therapist);
- *Couple* therapy (the two spouses together);
- *Family* therapy (several family members at the same time);
- *Group* therapy, or development of personal potential;
- **Within** *organizations* (schools, psychiatric hospitals, institutions for maladjusted youth, etc.);
- **In** *businesses*, industry and commerce, to improve contact and communication, enrich human relations, manage conflicts, and stimulate creativity.

Gestalt Therapy is not limited to those *suffering* from psychological, physical or psychosomatic difficulties. It also helps people faced with *existential problems*, which are, unfortunately, very common (conflict, separation, sexual problems, loneliness, bereavement, depression, unemployment, etc.). Gestalt can in fact be useful to *any person* (or group) seeking to develop hidden potential, not only *well-being* but also *"better-being"*, a better *quality of life*.

To summarize, Gestalt is a *natural, universal* approach, for people of all ages, all levels, from diverse cultural backgrounds and in a variety of situations. In fact, Perls considered his method too good to be reserved for the ill and the odd, and he often spoke of it, in a provocative manner, as *"therapy for normal people"*.

Gestalt Therapy: History and Geography

So what is this "new therapy", still incompletely defined for the public, and also known as *here-and-now therapy, contact therapy, existential psychoanalysis, integrative therapy, imaginary psychodrama* . . . and who knows what else?

By the 1980's, Gestalt had become one of the most widespread therapeutic, personal development and training methods in the USA. In some countries, it became as popular as psychoanalysis. In the USA, Gestalt is frequently taught to psychologists, social workers, ministers, youth workers and the Army. It is estimated that several hundreds of thousands of people have had individual or group sessions.

With its European roots, Gestalt rapidly became popular in Anglo-Saxon and Germanic countries. It is now continuing to spread over every continent: Canada, Latin America, Australia, Russia, Japan, etc. In Germany, Gestalt is taught in many institutes since 1969, and there are now over 2,000 professionals (including social workers, trainers, consultants, teachers, psychiatrists, psychologists—as well as Gestalt-pedagogues and Gestalt-gerontologists).

Gestalt Therapy: a brief presentation

Gestalt was developed from the intuitions of *Fritz Perls*, a Jewish psychoanalyst from Germany, who immigrated to the USA at the age of 53.

Gestalt Therapy was *conceived* with *Ego, Hunger and Aggression* Perls' first book. It was published in 1942, in South Africa, where Perls lived for a time during Nazi persecution.

Gestalt Therapy was born and *baptized* in 1951, when the book *Gestalt Therapy* was published in New York. The Gestalt movement grew slowly, and became famous much later in California, in 1968. The "hippies" were questioning the established value systems, and were seeking creativity ("Power to the imagination!") and responsibility for one's actions ("self-management"). It was time to emphasize *being* rather than *having*, *knowledge* instead of *power*.

Today, Gestalt rather than being just another psychotherapy, can be seen as a true *existential philosophy*, an "art of living" with authentic contact, and a way of looking at how we relate to the world.

Traditional priorities are often reversed: synthetic global view is valued over analytical approaches; looking to the future (finalism) is more important than looking for "causes" in the past; creativity and originality are emphasized, rather than normalization.

Perls and his colleagues (especially Laura Perls and Paul Goodman) had the genius to build a *coherent synthesis* of several philosophical, methodological and therapeutic methods, from *Europe, America and the East.* A new "Gestalt" was formed, where "the whole is different from the sum of its parts": by using traditional "bricks", a new and completely original structure was created (with the same bricks, one can build a prison or a cathedral . . .).

Gestalt is at the intersection of *psychoanalysis,* Reichian *body therapies* (from Wilhelm Reich, psychoanalyst and Freudian dissident), *psychodrama, phenomenological and existential approaches* and *Eastern* philosophies.

Gestalt develops a *unifying* vision of the human being, which integrates *senses, feelings, thought, social relationships and spirituality.* This paves the way towards a *holistic* experience, where the body can "speak" and words can be "seen and felt".

The emphasis is on *becoming aware of what is happening here and now* (present experience may of course include feelings about a past event). *Physical sensations and emotions* find their place: these are so often taboo in modern cultures, and lead towards strictly *controlled* public expression of anger, sadness, worry, but also affection, love and joy!

Authentic *contact* with others, *creative adjustment (creative adaptation of the organism to its environment),* and awareness of *repetitive* reactions and habits that are no longer useful can all be improved. Gestalt highlights these *blockages* in our *normal cycle* of need-fulfillment, it also highlights our avoidances, our fears, our inhibitions and our illusions.

Gestalt not only tries to *explain* why, it encourages *experimentation* with new *solutions* for old problems. It is not just a matter of "knowing why": Gestalt adds "feeling how", which motivates change.

In Gestalt therapy, each person is *responsible* for his own choices and avoidances. The individual works at the rate and level that suits him, according to what emerges in the present moment. He may see, hear or feel something, he may be preoccupied by a *current* problem or by unfinished business from the *past*; he may worry about the *future*. The session is *individualized*, and the client works on his own problem, even when in a group. The role of the group is to act as witness, to support, to amplify and provide feedback.

Gestalt integrates and combines many varied techniques in an original way: *verbal and non-verbal* methods, such as sensory awareness, working with energy, breathing, body or voice, emotional expression, dreams and waking dreams, psychodrama and creativity (drawing, modeling, music, dance, etc).

In summary, it is not a question of understanding, analyzing or interpreting events, behavior or feelings. What is important is to encourage global awareness of how we work, of our creative adjustment to the environment, of how we live and integrate our present experience, of our avoidances and our defense mechanisms ("avoidances" or "resistances", in the Gestalt sense).

A third way

This is a basic attitude that differs from the psychoanalytical and behavioral approaches; an original "third way": the point is not to understand nor to learn, but to *experiment*. This gives us a wider spectrum of experience, and allows greater freedom of choice. It also is a way out of *the alienating determinism of the past and the environment*, and an alternative to the historical or geographical conditioning that we have absorbed from our childhood and our surroundings. The result is a range of freedom and responsibility. To paraphrase Sartre:

> *"The important thing is not what others made of me,*
> *but what I make of what they made of me."*

It would be pointless to naïvely deny the weight of biological *heredity* or *early childhood experience*, or to ignore *social pressure*. It is rather a matter of seeking internal coherence of *who and how I am, globally, in the world*: to discover and develop my own style of living, which is *unique and personal*.

Gestalt encourages me, especially in the beginning, to get to *know myself better, and accept myself*, rather than trying to change myself to conform to some sort of *norm* (may it be individual or social, internal or external, philosophical, moral, religious or political).

To be as I am before being otherwise, this is what Beisser referred to in 1970 as the *"paradoxical theory of change"*.

In practice, such principles lead to a particular working style, based on *phenomenology* and certain techniques. Phenomenology, which preceded and contributed to existentialism, means looking at the immediate, subjective experience of each person. It is his personal description of the phenomenon, devoid of interpretation, based on his concrete feeling actually taking place "here-and-now": as opposed to the "objective" aims of behaviorism.

Unfortunately people still confuse the techniques (some borrowed from psychodrama, others subsequently used in other approaches such as Transactional Analysis) with actual Gestalt. Sometimes one hears "I'm doing Gestalt", by people who are largely ignorant of the fundamental principles—just because they use an "empty chair" or make someone talk to a cushion! . . . As if it would suffice to get someone to act to do psychodrama, or to lie on a couch to do psychoanalysis . . .

The most essential aspect of Gestalt Therapy is not the techniques themselves, but the general spirit that precedes and justifies them.

In Gestalt, a person's *symptom* is considered as his individual way to express himself, his "chosen language". The symptom is respected, and may even be temporarily *encouraged and exaggerated* using the *amplification* technique. Increasing the symptom can help the client[1] "hear" its message: what is my sore throat trying to say to me? The symptom, often physical, can serve as a channel, towards closer contact with the deep *sub-cortical* cerebral layers. *(see chapter 6)*.

In this type of work, the Gestalt therapist may *actively intervene*, but not directively. He can suggest or encourage; he *interacts* with the client. He does not impose an *aim or direction*: he places his professional capacity at the client's disposal, as would a mountain guide or speleology guide (who explores hidden depths) for example. The therapist *accompanies* the client on the road that *the client* chooses to explore. The therapist's role is to *facilitate*, rather than to understand or to make him do something.

The Gestalt practitioner and his client are *partners*, within an *authentic dual relationship*, which is exactly what characterizes Gestalt.

Ginger's Pentagram

To illustrate this *multidimensional* approach, I often use a *Pentagram*, or five-pointed star, which is the traditional, symbolic[2] image of Man—with his head, two arms and two legs.

The five branches represent for me the *five main dimensions* of human activity:

1) The **physical** dimension: body, senses, movement, physical sexuality . . .
2) The **emotional** dimension: "heart", feelings, love . . .
3) The **rational** dimension: "head" (with both hemispheres!), ideas, creativity, imagination . . .
4) The **social** dimension: other people, human and cultural environments . . .
5) The **spiritual** dimension: man's place in the cosmos and in the global ecosystem . . .

The two arms of the Pentagram deal with *relationship* (to our significant other, or to others in general), and the two legs symbolize our *roots*, which maintain the balance between physical and meta-physical, between matter and spirit (or energy). Disembodied spirituality is fragile or suspect.

Ginger's Pentagram (1983)

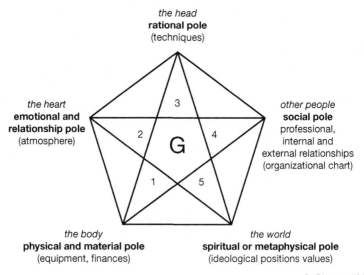

© Ginger, 1983

Gestalt Therapy strives to maintain its effective multidimensional approach, with a "polysemic" (many possible meanings) outlook, including these physical, emotional, rational, social and spiritual poles. It goes even further; it is not only these aspects which are important, but also the *interactions* between them. And this seems to us to be one of its main contributions. In fact it could even be said, in a simple, yet evocative way, that Gestalt restores *right-sided* globalizing brain function. In some "civilized" societies the left brain is so highly valued that we often become "hemiplegic", and are dependent on the analytical and rational functions of the left brain. Fortunately, in some countries, education is giving more time to artistic and physical activities.

Of course, this approach can be *extrapolated* from individuals to couples, families, organizations and companies. This diagram is a useful diagnostic and heuristic (discovery) aid, as it can point to problem areas and indicate appropriate, coherent strategies of intervention[3].

What I call "socio-Gestalt" is not Gestalt within an organization: it is the application of Gestalt principles to a whole organization (e.g. school, hospital, company), which may be considered to be a global "organism" in interaction with its environment[4].

Some techniques

To illustrate Gestalt to those who have not practiced it, let's have a quick look at some examples of the more common techniques used in Gestalt Therapy:

AMPLIFICATION

One of the major themes of Gestalt is to make *explicit* that which is *implicit*, to *bring out in the open* that which is hidden. When the client can *externalize* what is going on inside, he can see a clear picture of how he "works" here-and-now, and what goes on at the "contact boundary" between himself and his environment.

This process involves paying closer attention to "superficial phenomena" than to the obscure, hypothetical "depths" of the *unconscious*—which can only be explored with the use of interpretation: at best, a difficult tool; and at worst, sheds an artificial light. Gestalt is fundamentally attentive to the actual *process*.

For example, the phenomena of blushing of the face and neck are clues that may indicate emotion. Twitching in the jaw, rapid *breathing*, swallowing and all the *micro-movements* of hands and feet are other clues. Often the therapist will suggest *amplification* of such unconscious gestures, considered to be physical "Freudian slips", as they are likely to reveal something about the current process, hidden from the client himself.

The Gestalt-therapist starts *at the surface and works towards deeper levels*—which does not mean that he *stays* on the surface! In fact, experience has confirmed that Gestalt leads to deeper "archaic" layers of the personality more easily than other, more *verbal* approaches. Such archaic structures were formed during early development, before language was fully acquired.

MONODRAMA

This is a variant of *psychodrama* where the client *himself* takes the role, one by one, of *different characters* concerned. For instance, he could be himself, then his wife; then, his mother who rejects him coldly, followed by the same mother, now loving and present. He could speak as his rational mind and as his lustful penis, arguing with each other ("I must not seduce my colleague . . ." but "I really want to . . . "), and enact both of these states consecutively, in pre-conscious rivalry.

Monodrama allows exploration, recognition and integration of the opposing "polarities" in relationships, without getting arbitrarily "stuck in the middle": a false, artificial and arid middle way. I can in fact feel violently aggressive towards someone, *and* love him or her passionately, *at the same time*. Each of these feelings deserves to be *clarified* as much as possible and not just "neutralized" by a composite attitude of relative love, nor reduced to the "bland greyishness" which results from the arbitrary algebraic sum of two violent and opposing feelings. In fact, strong and opposing emotions are in reality more *additive* than canceling.

In contrast with the traditional quest of a *static*, narrow "middle way", Gestalt seeks to attain *dynamic* equilibrium. In the same way as a tightrope walker maintains his balance by *extending the breadth* of his pole, Gestalt encourages us to spread our wings, and open up to a *wider range of experiences*. We can trade in the gray blandness of compromise, for the colorful spectrum of the rainbow!

Gestalt Enactment

Enacting a real or imaginary scene, in a symbolic mode (without precise direction), can allow for expression, *abreaction* (emotional discharge, which can allow for liberation from the effects of a traumatic event) and finishing off "unfinished situations". Unfinished situations can lead to neurotic repetition, and consistently inappropriate or anachronistic "life scenarios" (such as sexual troubles in adulthood, long after the experience of abuse or rape).

Psychotherapeutic interventions do not aim to transform the *external* situation, or to change things, people or events. Instead, we work on transforming the *internal* perception of the client, and the way he perceives reality, relationships and the many possible meanings (polysemia) that exist: the client has the opportunity to change how he sees and interprets things, and to appreciate the diversity of interpretations for one "fact". Therapeutic work encourages exploration of *new and different personal experiences*, re-elaboration of the individual's system of perception, and a shift in the client's mental representation of his experience (reframing).

I would like to point out that this deliberate *symbolic enactment* of real or imaginary situations is the *opposite* of *impulsive or defensive acting out*. The latter is justly condemned by psychoanalysis: acting out is an *avoidance* of conscious realization (the act *replaces* verbal analysis), whereas *deliberate* enactment, on the contrary, is a way to *highlight* the process, encouraging conscious realization via visible and tangible (incarnate) action. The client's body and emotions are mobilized, which allows him to experience the situation in *all its intensity*, he can "re-present" it ("bring it into the present"), experiment and explore poorly identified, hidden or even unknown feelings.

Awareness

Awareness, or global consciousness, in Gestalt Therapy, signifies being continuously aware of the *ever-changing* continuum of physical sensations, emotions, ideas, and the uninterrupted succession of "figures". The figure, or form, is "that which I notice" out of the whole "background" or "ground" (made up of what I am doing and who I am, in every sense: physical, emotional, imaginary, rational, behavioral). The therapist himself is constantly in a state of *internal awareness* (aware of his own feelings) and *external awareness* (aware of what is going on in his environment, particularly with his client).

In Gestalt, we avoid speaking about a person, whether he is present or absent. Instead, we try to address him *directly*; this means that from an *intellectualized* internal *reflection*, we can proceed to *contact* in the relationship, with *feeling*. Thus, if I have something to say to my neighbor, I don't say "I think that Jane is . . .", but I speak to her directly ("Jane, when you do that, I feel so . . . "). Similarly, if I have harbored resentment against my deceased father, I can imagine that he is seated before me (on an empty chair, for instance) and I can speak to him face-to-face: "Dad, I never dared tell you that . . . "

In group therapy, the client is encouraged to verify his perceptions with the people concerned. This flushes out the ever-present, subtle *projections* with which we unconsciously protect ourselves. Such direct confrontation means that I will not blame my neighbor . . . for my own projections! For example: "I get the feeling you're not listening to me!"

I'll finish with these examples, because in fact, each therapist can continually *invent* new techniques, imagine variants and combine and adapt those described here. The varieties are endless, especially as each Gestaltist works with *who he is* as well as with what he *knows*; he develops his own style in his own personal *creative* way.

Gestalt, a therapy for our time

Gestalt is in tune with a new paradigm (way of thinking, system of beliefs) that demystifies the "all-powerful" status of scientific thought.

"The idea of man as completely rational is totally irrational."
(Edgar Morin)

The coldly objective science of the 19th century (which contributed to the development of psychoanalysis) has reached its limits, even in the so called "exact" sciences.

Chaos theory has revealed a "fractal" universe, which is infinitely complex and where *everything is a question of scale*. An object appears different according to the distance of the observer. For example, it is impossible to measure the "true" length of the California coastline: the closer one gets, the more irregularities are visible, and the true length thus approaches infinity! As predicted by Gestalt, what you see *depends on how you look,* and how you look *influences what you see.*

Each person has his own truth. Subjectivity means that the subject "inhabits" the object, breathes life into it.

It is clear today that:

- Intuitive *synthesis* precedes rational analysis,
- Clarifying the desired *aim* can be more helpful than understanding the past *causes,*
- The optimistic *finalism* of "what for" wins over the pessimistic *causalism (causation)* of "why",
- The creative "poetry" (from the Greek *poïeïn,* "to create") has overtaken the stereotypical, "mathematical" rigidity of matter (from the Greek *mathema,* "what is written").

Therefore, in contrast to psychoanalysis, Gestalt does not claim to be a *science,* but takes pride in remaining an *art*—and in the process, joins with the progression of modern research: in physics, biology and philosophy, all are seeking unification of matter and energy, of body and spirit.

Notes

1. In Gestalt, people are referred to as "clients" rather than "patients": the latter has a passive and medical connotation, whereas the former indicates that the person is active in the therapeutic engagement, free and responsible in his search and choices.
2. "Symbolic" as opposed to "diabolic", from the Greek *dia-boleïn* which means "throw about, separate" while *sun-boleïn* means "throw together, assemble". Symbolic language brings all peoples together, and is like a natural "phylogenetic esperanto".
3. Try this test! See how your couple works, according to each pole: physical, emotional, intellectual, social, spiritual . . .
4. Try the same test for your workplace: concrete (equipment), relationships (atmosphere), rational (technology), social (hierarchical structure, and contact with the outside world), ideology (guiding principles) . . .

CHAPTER TWO

The Therapist is incarnate

The duty to be happy

After this overview, what can we recall about Gestalt therapy?

Gestalt therapy concerns us all. It can help us to identify blockages and difficulties, to explore new ways of functioning, to tame our fears, doubts and suffering. The accent today is on preventive medicine: there is no need to await suffering before seeking help. We have seen that Gestalt is, above all, the constant search for harmony and a better quality of life. Each of us has a right to happiness.

We have been brought up to believe that we must "earn the right to happiness". There is no reward without effort: "No pain, no gain"; "Life was not meant to be easy." The fast track to sainthood is virginity and martyrdom! Spirituality is easily nourished by asceticism.

Is this in fact true? It is not so easy to prove it. *"There are many roads to wisdom"*, say the Oriental Sufis, *"Seek, and seek joyfully . . . "*

What is the use of making your knuckles bleed in removing every stone from your garden? There will always be more, despite our best efforts; what is the point of wearing ourselves out, if there will always be stones no matter how hard we dig? What about using that energy to *water the flowers?* Or to plant some . . . even in the rock garden!

Obviously, it is easier to develop what we already have (the gift of music, sport, or easy contact) rather than struggle in vain against "negative" characteristics (stop smoking, being less lazy, less proud, etc). No therapeutic pathway can bypass tears and anxiety, but is it truly valid and useful to spend so much time over difficulties from the past? Especially as it is possible, at the same time, to cultivate the present and concentrate on maximizing one's potential for happiness.

Clients in Gestalt are often surprised to discover that it is possible to "work on" success, good contact and well-being, and not just problem areas or traumatic events. In fact, continually going over a painful moment often serves to reinforce the bad memory; continually talking about a difficult period of mourning is not enough to overcome it . . . Reopening the wounds of childhood and making them bleed means they will never get a chance to heal: *once the wound is properly cleaned* (but not before!) there is a necessary convalescence while the scab forms and must not be scratched off. This type of "first aid" is often painful; but calming creams, tenderness and humor are part of every treatment.

Avoid neither suffering, nor joy. Gestalt psychotherapy aims for the flourishing of the being. Let's not cultivate certain *masochistic* tendencies which imply that the greater the cost, the suffering and the duration of the therapy, the more it is "deep and valid"! "Not expensive – not good"! "Not long = not deep"! are tenacious myths!

At the market, when the *very same sack* of potatoes is divided between 3 baskets labeled 1, 2 and 3 dollars, most people ask for the most expensive! A recent American meta-analysis of 80 studies dealing with the real effects of various therapies showed no significant correlation between length, price and results, neither in the short term nor the long term . . .

When the cellar is cleared of the *most cumbersome* objects, it is time to renovate the ground level and enjoy the house. Once there, it is possible to relax and recuperate. One can always go back down to clean up some more, later on, bit by bit.

> "The most we can do for those we love, is to be happy ourselves."
> Alain *(Propos sur le Bonheur)*

In this way, those we love receive the gift of our presence, which is open and bright. Let us not weigh them down with our devotion or sacrifice. Our inner sun extends its warmth to them. It is no longer a question of "a right to happiness" but indeed a "duty to be happy."

Controlled involvement and sympathy

Gestalt advocates letting go, and trust. The aim of this is to accompany the client in the "need satisfaction cycle" *(see chap. 4)*. This can be done with warmth and sharing, which always helps growth, and without exaggerating the role of frustration as the way to progression.

The therapist in Gestalt is not walled up in stony silence; he does not hide behind a mask of permanent "benevolent neutrality". He will show *sympathy*, share his ideas and feelings (put his counter-transference to therapeutic use), and interact with his client as a partner. Of course, his involvement is *measured* and he does not express *everything* he feels . . . but what he does express, he truly feels (he maintains a fundamentally *authentic* relationship). To put it simply: he thinks all he says, but does not say all he thinks.

The therapist is not obliged to accept the client unconditionally: he may refuse the client's propositions. Such an original therapeutic standpoint is Gestalt-specific: the therapist is there for the client, but not to do anything at all, or to go just anywhere! If I want to go over my reactions to my mother's suicide for the thirtieth time, the therapist can suggest an *experimental alternative*: "What if this time, you told me about a happy moment with her, when you were little?" Too much repetition can rigidify: explore, go over, yes; eternal rumination, no. On the other hand, if I systematically avoid bringing up difficult situations, the therapist will not hesitate to help me become aware of this.

Perls caricaturized three basic therapeutic "positions":

- **Psychoanalytic** "a-pathy": benevolent neutrality, with minimal involvement and little intervention;
- **Rogerian** "em-pathy" (Carl Rogers): the therapist puts himself in the client's shoes, to understand and feel with him;
- **Gestaltist** "sym-pathy": the therapist is present as an attentive, competent partner, using a real "I/Thou" dialogue (Buber). If I am angry, my therapist can stay calm; I can be sad, and he, not . . .

Exploring together

The therapist is not "supposed to know" everything about me. I am a *unique, original* person and I maintain the right to my own personal style of functioning. My needs and my lacks are not those of another, and my reactions to my father's absence differ from those of my brother . . .

Even if my Gestalt therapist has studied extensively (it takes around *10 years*, including *personal psychotherapy*, basic *training* and *supervised practice*), even if he has wide experience of human nature and difficulties, he knows nothing about *my* inner self. He is like a speleology guide, who knows how to explore hidden depths . . . discovering, for the *first* time, *my own*.

> The therapist gives me the security of his practice, the help of his technique and equipment, and he discovers—*at the same time as I do*—my originality. He respects my differences, just as he respects *my willingness to explore, and my daily limits.* While I determine the itinerary, he accompanies me *without imposing rhythm or circuit.* Nevertheless, he assures my safety and may refuse a dangerous or premature journey. He can also comment on the sites, spectacular or otherwise, and point out useless detours or *avoidances.* After the expedition, this mutual discovery, he can help me draw a map and assess the situation. Putting the experience into words helps to signpost the emotions that appeared along the way, and allows easier orientation for the next time.

Bringing the word to life

In traditional verbal therapies, words precede emotion. In Gestalt, on the other hand, verbalization often *springs from* feeling:

I feel a sort of pressure, I imagine an enormous vice squashing my chest (*the therapist intensifies this sensation by squeezing my body with his arms*), I am surprised to find myself screaming and fighting him off, "Get away from me! I can't breathe! Let me get some air! . . . I need to get away . . . alone, even for just a few days, on holiday . . ."

As we can see, the Gestalt therapist may intervene verbally or physically—if he feels it is useful to *intensify the process* and allow the client *himself* to discover what the situation means to him; to find his own personal meaning.

It is only afterwards that I will analyze—with the therapist—the significance (or various possible meanings) of what automatically "came out of my mouth." I will be able to see how much my present life (personal or professional) reproduces and awakens the poignant feelings hidden away since childhood, which continued to develop during adolescence. It is important to note that it is not this *realization* alone which will change everything for me. It is the *experience*, even symbolic and temporary, of a different position (such as, I freed myself from the vice-like grip of my therapist) that is important. Each experience is recorded, or "engrammed" in the deep layers of the limbic brain, as new neural pathways are created *(see ch. 6)*.

Gestalt is often used in *group therapy*, where the group generally acts as a support (which may be interactive) for the dual interaction between the therapist and the client. Sometimes group members are called to participate. In this form of Gestalt group therapy, each person "works on" his issues *when he desires*, before the group: for a time ranging from minutes to half an hour or more.

Another application of Gestalt to group work is "Gestalt *of* the group," which is centered on actual interactions between group members, and is similar to traditional group dynamic approaches. This approach is particularly interesting *within an already-formed group*, such as in organizations, where the interpersonal relationships depend not only on each individual, but also on the character and history of the organization itself.

This chapter has shown that Gestalt psychotherapy is not really "individual" or "group" therapy, but is in fact "dual" therapy. The therapist[1] is involved as well as the client: the therapeutic relationship draws on what happens in the present time between the two partners,[2] including the unpredictable nature of the contact, as well as what it means. The focus is on becoming conscious or aware of the current process, as well as experimentation with different ways of being: within this context, new internal and external standpoints can be explored, in a creative and well-adjusted[3] way.

Notes

1. Who has analyzed his own attitudes at length during his basic training, and who continues to do so with regular supervision.

2. What actually happens in the session often corresponds surprisingly well with the client's current theme. For example, when the client talks about her passivity when faced by her "overprotective" mother during childhood, it would not be unusual to find a similar passive submission to the therapist's suggestions ("transference").

3. *See ch. 4* for discussion of *creative adjustment*.

CHAPTER THREE

Fritz Perls, the Father of Gestalt Therapy

Recognized at last, at 75 years old!

"*Iinvented nothing,*" said Perls, "*all I did, was rediscover what was always there.*" In fact, the Gestalt "revolution" is simply opening our eyes to daily phenomena. The practical applications of this had been neglected:

- We all know that each of us perceives our world from our own personal perspective, yet we continue to seek in vain a so-called "scientific" objectivity . . .
- We also know that our emotions often get the best of us, and we continue to act as if our head always ruled our heart . . .
- We have all heard that you cannot judge a book by its cover, and fail to appreciate the significance of the cover itself . . .
- We all know that "how" is more important than "why," and that the spirit in which something is done is important, (as sung by Brassens, "the way she passed us the bread, we received cake") but we are still mostly interested in the "bottom line" . . .
- We are similarly aware that it is possible to break away from the past, just as Demosthenes, despite his stammer, became a great speaker . . .

We know all this with our own experience, but therapeutic methods have failed to reap the consequences.

True to the pattern of many geniuses, Fritz Perls was an unusual person who did not fit into society. He was not afraid to flaunt his difference, and did so whenever he could. He scorned social norms and politeness, and always said exactly (often brutally) what he felt: he was progressively rejected by many colleagues because of this behavior. He did not claim to be either a sage or prophet, and even pretended to be ignorant and uneducated (despite degrees in medicine and philosophy). The conservative social climate in which he lived, America in the 50s, was certainly unable to accept his attitude of provocative liberalism. And so, at the age of 72, he was an unknown, worn out, semi-retired old man.

With the "1968 revolution" (he was 75) Perls was finally "discovered" by a journalist and made the front page of *Life* magazine. Glory at last! *"This is a man who embodies authenticity, and who practices what he preaches!"* The public responded, ready and waiting for such a man, who represented a return to human values, after the invasion of cold technology.

Each weekend, Perls gave talks and demonstrations about a new way of life, free and "embodied," with fast, deep, direct contact. In only a few minutes, he could identify each person's existential issue and suggest ways to help. The best East Coast psychologists traveled over 3,000 miles to go to "the show."

Gestalt therapy jumped from obscurity to the front page, and Perls became the "father figure" of this new technique—which would progressively reach every continent: from America to Australia, from Japan to Russia . . . and that's not the end!

A journey of ups and downs

Friedrich Salomon Perls (who was later called Fritz) was born in an obscure part of the Jewish ghetto in Berlin, in 1893[1].

His father was a wine merchant, and his frequent journeys were the occasion for multiple love affairs. He despised his son and called him a "pile of shit" . . . Fritz hated him back and did not even go to his funeral! Throughout his lifetime, Fritz rebelled against every paternal figure (including Freud) and he fought for anarchic groups.

His mother was a practicing Jew who loved opera and the theatre (a love shared by Fritz, throughout his whole life). She often fought with her husband, and they were also known to physically hit each other.

A "bad" boy

By the age of 10, Fritz was intolerable: he refused to learn his lessons, he falsified his reports, he tore up the whip used by his mother and threw it in her face . . . he was expelled from school when he was 13. His rebelliousness did not take long to appear.

His father found him an apprenticeship, but Fritz decided on his own to enroll in a liberal school where he resumed his studies. At the same time, he became very active in expressionist theatre in a "left-inspired" group, which advocated *complete commitment* of the actor to his role. Later in New York, Fritz was a regular visitor to the *Living Theatre*. Gestalt allowed him to develop his taste for acting, as well as total involvement of the actors . . . and also for independent anarchy!

His studies were interrupted by World War I, where he was gassed and wounded in the trenches at the front.

After the war, he finished his medical degree, and went on to specialize in neuropsychiatry at the age of 27.

Four psychoanalyses

When he was 33, Perls began his first psychoanalysis, with Karen Horney. She would continue to support him throughout his life, and welcomed him to New York, twenty years later.

At the same time he worked as a medical assistant with Kurt Goldstein, whose research interest was for perceptive disorders after neurological lesions: much of his work was based on Gestalt psychology. Fritz met Laura, his future wife, here; she became a psychoanalyst herself and actively participated in the development of their new method.

Perls went through three subsequent analyses before setting up analytical practice himself.

His third analyst, Eugen Harnik was especially strict: he maintained a permanent attitude of distant neutrality, and even refused to shake his client's hands. He never spoke more than one phrase per week, and instead of announcing the end of the session (which would reveal his tone of voice), he scratched the floor with his foot! Perls continued his daily analysis for 18 months. In keeping with orthodox analysis, Harnik forbade any important decisions during the analytical cure (to avoid undue influence from the effects of treatment). So when Fritz decided to marry, he had to stop analysis and "exchanged with joy the analytical couch for the marital bed"! He was 36 years old at the time; Laura was 24.

His fourth analysis was much less classical. Wilhelm Reich, who was to become one of Freud's dissidents, and who led the way to bioenergetics, practiced an *active* technique. He would frequently touch his clients, to help them become aware of their tensions. He would easily bring up issues relating to sexuality (as he considered orgasm as a central balancing factor) and aggression, and was militant for liberal Marxism (which led to his exclusion from the communist party). He would soon be asked to leave from the international psychoanalytical Society due to his "excessive involvement". Perls retained great respect for his analyst, and his Gestalt Therapy includes many Reichian principles.

In 1934, when he was 41 years old, Perls left Nazi Germany for South Africa, where he founded the South African Psychoanalytic Institute. He followed *traditional* practice, with five 50-minute sessions each week, and with no patient contact. Later he said that he had become a "calculating cadaver, just like most analysts of the time". Nevertheless he developed a considerable clientele, and became rich and famous: he lived on a magnificent property, with a tennis court, a swimming pool and even a skating rink! He piloted his own airplane and led a bourgeois, celebrity lifestyle with Laura.

Schism

Two years later, the rupture took place: Perls traveled to the *International Psychoanalytic Conference* in Marienbad, where he gave a paper on *oral resistances*. He maintained that the *hunger* instinct is as central as the sexual instinct, and that *aggression* is essential to survival, and appears as first teeth break through. This reading received cold criticism from his colleagues. Freud said no more than a few words to him, and Reich barely recognized him, despite their work in analysis, every day, for over two years! Perls was very offended, and would remain for ever hostile towards his former teachers.

On returning to South Africa, Perls wrote his first book *Ego, Hunger and Aggression*, which was published in 1942. The first edition was sub-titled *"A revision of Freud's Theory"* ... but Freud, as we know, disliked criticism! This book contains the elements of what would become Gestalt Therapy, nine years later: the importance of here and now, the role of the body, direct contact, respecting feelings, global approach, patient responsibility, etc.

America

After the Second World War, in 1946, Perls decides to leave everything: his family, his well-established practice, and his wealthy clients. He leaves looking for adventure and a new life in the USA. In New York, he sets up practice once again as an analyst, albeit somewhat "deviant," and continues to respect traditional principles such as use of the couch, and verbal, non-physical work. He will therefore have worked for 23 years as a *psychoanalyst* before he officially inaugurates his new method in 1951, at the age of 58.

In New York, he resumes a bohemian lifestyle, similar to that of his youth. He frequents "left-wing intellectuals," writers and "New Age" theatrical people. He is a regular at the *Living Theatre*, which advocates immediate expression of feelings, via direct, spontaneous contact with the public, and prefers improvisation to traditional rote learning and rehearsals.

Laura comes to join Fritz in New York, and every Wednesday night they host the *Group of Seven*. This group includes Paul Goodman (a controversial writer, who will later organize Perl's writings), Isadore From (a phenomenological philosopher who would make known the Self Theory), Paul Weisz (who initiates Perls to Zen), etc.

Gestalt Therapy is officially recognized

The Gestalt "Bible" *Gestalt Therapy,* based on Perls' notes, is written by Paul Goodman in 1951. The book, difficult to read, is not successful, and only a few hundred copies are sold. It would not become well known until *twenty years later*, thanks to Isadore From, when Gestalt therapy was finally "taking off."

In 1952, Perls, his wife, Goodman and From begin teaching this new method in two small centers, one in New York, the other near Chicago, in Cleveland. There are few students, success is limited, and Perls attempts to publicize his approach by giving a series of nation-wide lectures, all the way from Canada, to California, and Florida.

Late-blooming love

It is 1956: Perls is worn out with preaching to dead ears. He and Laura grow apart; Fritz smokes three packs a day and he has heart trouble. At 63 years old, he feels that he has always been mis-understood, and is fed up with the general indifference of the population. He decides to retire to sunny Miami, and rents a small, dingy flat. He lives alone, dismal and without company; he has a few clients in therapy, but no friends. He remains sexually inactive, due to fear of heart attack . . .

And then it happens! Marty, a young woman of 32, falls in love with him. This love awakens his tired, old-man energy, and two years of passionate, belated happiness begins . . . until Marty finally leaves him for a younger lover!

Fritz then resumes his nomadic lifestyle of old, and travels from town to town to give conferences and demonstrate his technique. At the age of 70, he completes an around-the-world journey in 18 months, including a visit to a "Beatnik" village of young artists in Israel. He is fascinated by their confident, libertarian attitude to life, and is inspired to take up his brushes and paint. Then he flies to Japan where he spends several months in a Zen monastery . . . but without attaining *satori*, his hoped-for illumination. He returns in disappointment.

California

In April 1964, Perls sets up practice in Esalen, south of San Francisco. Esalen is now famous, and is known as the "Mecca of humanistic psychology." Two young Americans, enthralled with psychology and Orientalism, had just opened a Center for Development of Human Potential, to which they invited well-known speakers to lead seminars and workshops.

Fritz holds many Gestalt workshops here, but his hour of glory has not yet arrived; only 4 or 5 people came to each session!

Finally the worldwide 1968 Hippie movement began, starting with Californian students who were fed up with the "American way of life." What is the use of getting rich, if you are not happy? The never-ending hunt for "having more and more" gives way to a search for "just being, and becoming better": it is a question of quality of life. Suits and ties are abandoned in favor of faded jeans, big factories give way to cottage industries (working from home, in small groups, would open the way for computers and telecommunications to develop). It is the time of *Small is Beautiful, Paradise Now, Forbidding is Forbidden, Art for the People* . . .

Life magazine publishes an issue presenting Perls, and his search for authenticity in relationship, unhampered by pretense. Suddenly his audience "explodes": with over 300 people each day, only a lucky few are able to spend several minutes working directly with Fritz. He is the first to show spectacular new techniques where the client converses with himself in public: he gets up on stage, sits on the "hot seat," and facing an empty chair he talks to his spouse, child, father, etc (or rather, he talks to the internal image he has of them):

"Mum, why did you have to go and die so young? You left me when I needed you so badly, I'm very upset with you . . . "

Perls notes the tone of voice, the posture, the look, and the process of the imagined conversation, more than what is actually said. Speaking with himself, or with Fritz, the client becomes aware of whole aspects of his personality which have been hidden away, camouflaged as *introjections* (what I was taught to believe—which is not necessarily the same as what I feel deep down. For instance: "I could not resent a poor, sick person" or "Men don't cry", etc.), or held back, *retroflected*.

His lectures are videotaped, and one is published: *Gestalt Therapy Verbatim*, in 1969. This adds to the fame of the new method, and many specialists travel for the privilege of seeing Perls at work. They try out his methods, and borrow some of his ideas or techniques: Gregory Bateson (founder of the Palo Alto School), Alexander Lowen (founder of bio-energy), Eric Berne (creator of Transactional Analysis: TA), John Lilly (inventor of "sensory deprivation tanks"), Stanislav Grof (experimenter of LSD, creator of "holotropic breathing" and founder of transpersonal psychotherapy), John Grinder and Richard Bandler (founders of Neuro-Linguistic Programming, NLP), etc.

Gestalt-Kibbutz

Perls decides to found a community, or "kibbutz", where "Gestalt can be experienced 24 hours a day." Having moved from individual Gestalt Therapy to group work, he continues with Gestalt in daily life. He buys an old fisherman's motel on Vancouver Island, on Canada's West Coast, and moves in with some faithful followers. Everyone spends his time between therapy, training and collective tasks. Perls describes himself as "happy and contented at last".

His happiness is short-lived: the following winter, upon returning from Europe in March 1970, he has a heart attack and dies. And so he ended his long, and particularly unusual journey.

Some things to think about, from Perls' life:

- **A genius is rarely "adapted" to his environment:**

  "The only way to assert ourselves is through opposition" (Wallon).

- **Some geniuses are recognized at an early age, others, like Perls, much later on: Perls was 75 years old when he received recognition!**
- **Gestalt Therapy germinated in the mind of a German Jewish medical doctor, who was an analyst for 23 years: Gestalt Therapy is neither American nor ignorant of Psychoanalysis!**
- **A new theory can achieve widespread acceptance only when the environment is ready for it.**

Notes

1. For a more detailed biography, refer to: S. & A. GINGER, *La Gestalt, une thérapie du contact* (op. cit.)

CHAPTER FOUR

The Theory of the Self

A self . . . which does not exist!

U p to now, we have touched on underlying *principles* as well as some fundamental therapeutic *attitudes* in Gestalt. We have discussed neither *theory, method* nor *techniques* of this new approach, and in fact we will not go into detail here, as this book is not written specifically for Gestalt professionals[1], but for the public at large and potential clients.

A theory[2], in fact, neither explains nor represents "reality"; a theory is an organized, methodical, intellectual *construction*. It is *hypothetical* and synthetic, and elaborated for didactic reasons. Its principal aim is thus to offer a *provisional* interpretation, to provide a *coherent* framework for facts and phenomena: so that we can more easily apprehend, or predict events. Theories do not have to be *true*, but a good theory is *useful* and *easy to use*.

So, there will be no detailed historical presentation here, nor debates on current evolution, competing schools of thought, and subtle differences between authors. It is sufficient to briefly describe what convention calls *"Theory of the Self,"* which includes a definition of the *self* and its functions, a glimpse of creative adjustment at the contact boundary, and of the contact *cycle* and its blockages, interruptions or resistances, (or "defenses"). This theory comes mainly from Book 2 of *Gestalt Therapy* (1951), written by Paul Goodman from Fritz Perls' handwritten notes, and popularized—much later—by Isadore From (who died in June 1994).

28

It's about the *theory* of a notion—the *self*—which does not even exist! Neither you, nor I, have a *self*—in the Gestalt sense! The *self* has little to do with the Freudian *Ego*, the Jungian *Self*, the Transactional Analytical *Adult*, and it is similarly unrelated to Winnicott's *self*. It is not about me, but about *my way of being*, at this exact moment, in this exact place; it deals with current phenomena at the contact boundary between my immediate environment and myself. It deals with my present style of "creative adjustment," in a determined *field*. My *self* is thus eminently variable and intimately linked to a phenomenological world vision, which favors the subjective, temporal *process* over the establishment of permanent, objective human qualities.

That is as much as we will say here on such essential, yet philosophical and technical considerations. It is sufficient to rapidly go over the more concrete consequences that will come up constantly in one or other of the four complementary fields of Gestalt Therapy:

- *Individual* (dual) therapy,
- Personal development *groups*,
- Gestalt as practiced in *organizations*,
- Its application in commercial and industrial *businesses*.

The contact cycle

"Nevertheless, it turns!" cried Galileo, as he stood before the skeptical judges of the Inquisition. No one today doubts that *everything* in the Universe *turns* or *spins*: from electrons in their minute atomic "orbits," to planets and galaxies.

The wind is turning, chance also, as does the destiny of people and theories; everything is *cyclical*, from seasons to the ages of life. Our "internal biological clock" (coordinated by the *epiphysis*, or pineal gland—which regulates sleep, digestion, ovulation . . . and "jet-lag") is responsible for cycles including cardiac rhythm, temperature, hormone secretion, mood, as well as daily, monthly and seasonal activities.

Each experience has a *cycle* too: something begins, follows through and ends. Our whole life is an interwoven complex of cycles, one inside the other, like Russian dolls. You began to read this book, are continuing this very instant, and will soon finish; this is within the cycle of your whole day, itself within the week, and so on: in parallel, the bodily cycles are superimposed, as are the cycles of your love life, your professional activities, and your social or political engagements.

At any moment, a "dominant figure" emerges and occupies the foreground while the rest fades into the background. Thus, while absorbed in reading, you "forget" all about your sore back—which passes into the background. The foreground captures your interest, to the detriment of the background. This is the permanent *foreground/ background*, or *figure /ground* alternation, already highlighted in *Gestalt Psychology*, in the beginning of the century.

Gestalt Therapy has taken this fundamental human function into consideration. And so, Perls, Hefferline and Goodman (1951) proposed to divide each experience in *four* main time frames, organized around the notion of *contact*: forecontact, contacting, full contact (or "final contact") and post-contact. Such subdivision of every action certainly simplifies matters . . . but cannot take into consideration all observed phenomena.

Following this, other authors sought to refine the process to bring it into line with various concrete, real-life situations: from the "mini-cycle" of satisfaction of physical needs like hunger or thirst, right up to long and complex cycles such as the evolution of love relationships or professional careers.

Joseph Zinker (1977) identifies, for example, six phases: sensation, awareness, energy mobilization, action, contact and withdrawal.

Michel Katzeff (1978) adds a phase of completion (closure), before the withdrawal.

I personally prefer to distinguish *five* essential stages (*see diagram*):

1) Forecontact
2) Engagement
3) Contact ("full contact" or "final contact")
4) Disengagement
5) Assimilation of the experience.

Two of these stages merit particular attention: those which precede or immediately follow full contact. The cycle's success or failure depends to a great extent on these two phases, which I have called *engagement* and *disengagement*.

The Five Stages of the Contact Cycle (S. Ginger, 1989)

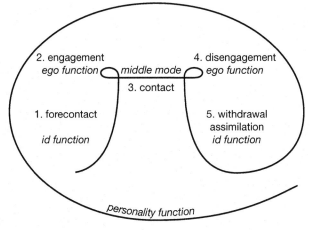

© S. Ginger, 1989

This outline that I propose evokes the Greek letter *pi*—which symbolizes, for me, the way to get from the circle's diameter to its perimeter, from the straight line to the cycle, from a project to its completion.

The two *loops* highlight the critical moments in the cycle, those *brief* instants where action begins and ends, just before assimilation.

What has become evident to me, after some experience, is that difficulties—as much the *client's* as the *therapists*—are mostly found in these two *key moments* of the cycle: just *prior to*, and just *after* the contact phase, i.e. at the moment of *contacting* and *before* withdrawal.

And thus, a *five*-stage cycle appears:

1) FORECONTACT

Most Gestalt authors have already *substantially developed* the necessity of a time of *forecontact*. This allows the time for a need, a desire, a project or a situation to *appear*. In order to be enriching, a meeting needs to be preceded by some informal exchange; making love implies time to let the desire mount, followed by the preliminaries. Commercial selling requires some time to put the client at ease; personal development work in Gestalt is preceded by a latent period, during which the client prepares himself for the "therapeutic alliance" . . . The absence of forecontact (or its excessive prolongation) indicates a psychological or social dysfunction (sometimes psychotic).

2) ENGAGEMENT

The moment of *contacting*, so very important, is often underestimated: this is a key moment where action is "consolidated," when one engages in a particular pathway of exploration in a therapeutic sequence, or when one commits to a relationship, to a group, a decision or a project.

This is why I call this stage *engagement*. This word seems very explicit to me, as it evokes the beginning of a defined interaction (troops engage in a battle, gears engage together, engagement traditionally precedes marriage). It is interesting to note that *engagement* is not always conscious, and does not always occur in a state of *awareness*; it does not always require the mobilization of energy: sometimes it is the result of intuition, of a progressive "slipping," or on the contrary, a sudden overbalance. Whatever it is, we're committed, and off we go! Whatever the reasons or justifications, there is that moment where "right, we're off, away we go!"; identifying and deliberately utilizing this critical moment seems to me to be essential.

3) CONTACT ("FINAL CONTACT" OR "FULL CONTACT")

Contact itself may, without a doubt, be subdivided into several sequences—the order of which may of course vary according to the situation. However I do not believe that going into detail in either therapeutic or clinical practice contexts is important: "whatever happens, happens," with highs and lows, and there is time to reflect upon whether the current phase involves orientation (a moment of choice), action or interaction . . .

4) DISENGAGEMENT

The other essential moment to manage is that of "disengagement": that point when the situation "resolves" itself in one way or another, where in any case, the current phase has ended, and it is time to observe the consequences, temporary or otherwise. *Before* the *withdrawal* phase, prior to the long period of assimilation, or digestion—conscious and unconscious—of the experience, there is a crucial moment at the end: stopping, separation, conclusion. The point at which the evening ends, when the lovers will separate, when the client leaves his therapist (until the next session . . . or definitively). These *significant parting moments mark out our whole lives*: we finish a conference, leave a meeting; we also leave our parents' house, finish our studies, quit work or a political party, divorce, move house, retire . . . At such moments, we are not in full contact, we are *not yet* in withdrawal, we are in the *critical moment of disengagement*—which may last minutes, days . . . or years (see "bereavement").

In daily life as in therapeutic practice, I have noticed that it is often a difficult moment, poorly "negotiated," uselessly *postponed* or awkwardly *precipitated*. In fact this phase, so important in every cycle seems to me to be insufficiently highlighted in traditional Gestalt Therapy theory. It merits more attention, and is generally the stumbling block for beginner therapists . . . and for many seasoned politicians!

5) WITHDRAWAL

I shall not spend too much time on what is—for me—the fifth phase of the cycle: *withdrawal*, in the sense that this is *assimilation*, or digestion. Most authors have highlighted its importance and none deny that training or psychotherapy—just like love—depends just as much on the time *between* encounters, as on the encounters themselves.

To summarize, engagement and disengagement are not lengthy periods, but are brief, delicate, decisive moments, which are easy to distinguish; an analogy I like is the take-off and landing of an airplane. The disengagement phase is especially important to point out: this stage precedes withdrawal and must not be confused with it. This stage is particularly important, especially as subsequent assimilation of the experience depends so much on it.

The "functions of the self"

During these different stages of "the Experiential Cycle" or "Contact Cycle," my *self* (i.e. my style of adapting to, and of interacting with, the environment) is ever changing. It "works" in *four main modes* or styles, that are traditionally called the "functions of the self": the "id," the "personality," the "ego" and the "middle mode." Each of these terms has a specific meaning in Gestalt Therapy:

- The **id** expresses the world of sensation, *needs* (conscious and unconscious) and urges: hunger, fatigue, and sexual desire. It just happens to me, regardless of what I may decide.
- The **personality** is the "foundation" from which desire emerges: this is what is *permanent* in me, my personal history, my background, which allows me to see myself as "someone who usually does this or that . . . ." It is my self-image, how I see myself, and particularly how I describe myself: "I am a man who . . . ." The *personality* manifests itself *before* and *after* each "cycle": the cycle depends on it, and the personality becomes richer from the cycle. Each experience, once assimilated, updates my self-image.
- The **ego** concerns my conscious and deliberate choices, for which I take full responsibility and which allow me to behave in a particular way. Depending on my *current* needs, and on my *on-going* personality, I make decisions (this ego function depends on both the *id* and the *personality*). It is a question of what *I want*, of what I decide today, in the present environment, in the present experiential *field*.
- The "**middle mode**" refers to Greek verb conjugation: neither active nor passive, but both at once. This mode has more or less disappeared from the English language; one persistent example would be "address oneself to." Similarly, when *we* speak to *each other*, in a "dialogue-type" interaction: it is full contact, mutual exchange between I and Thou, or between myself and my environment.

  Psychosis is usually linked to a disturbance of the *id* and *personality* functions, particularly active at the beginning and end of the cycle (forecontact and assimilation); neurosis is usually related to a disturbance of the *ego* mode.

Resistances

In practice, the contact cycle does not always progress regularly. There may be *interruptions*, slips, jumps, reversals, etc. These disturbances are usually called "resistances" in Gestalt. There are *five main ones: confluence, introjection, projection, retroflection, deflection* (some authors add *proflection, egotism, invalidation*, etc.). In fact, most function as "defense mechanisms," i.e. temporary *safety* reflexes, but which have become *excessive*, maladapted or *anachronistic*: thus, my coat of armor, which is supposed to protect me, has become too heavy, and is more of a cumbersome weight than a useful protection. Gestalt encourages me to *identify* and sort out those mechanisms which are helpful from those which are no more. With Gestalt Therapy, I can let go of those which are unnecessary, or simply change my rigid "coat of armor" into "chain mail," which is more flexible and better adapted.

Let's look at some common examples:

- **Confluence** is *pathological* if there is no boundary between another and myself: if my wife accompanies me to every ball game and if I always go shopping with her, our partnership becomes "fusionnal" where no-one knows who wants what. However, confluence may be *healthy* if I share my enthusiasm for a team, the delight in a family affair such as a birthday, or the struggle of my political party. This healthy confluence must not overflow the established limits: otherwise there is a slip-up: if for instance I vote the same way as the team captain, if my political party imposes a strict dress code, or if I blindly obey a guru or sect.

- **Introjection** is what "I have swallowed whole, without chewing or digesting." Some of these are necessary to live comfortably in society: I learned that it is important to have respect for others' possessions and for their well-being, to arrive on time for meetings, to not yell and shout in the street ... But I also "introjected" that it was wrong to masturbate (whereas we know today that it is a normal part of sexual development), that I had to be quiet and do what my parents and schoolmasters said—at the price of putting a stop to my progress! And why not reveal myself, in my *uniqueness* and with *assertiveness* (behavior of one who affirms himself with his assertions, without excessive timidity or boasting, in a correct manner at the right time). In fact, many of my childhood introjections weigh me down, instead of helping me to live a freer life.

- **Projection** is attributing things which concern myself, to another (often to unconsciously get rid of it): "You seem annoyed tonight" may cover up my own annoyance, just as "I'm sure you're going to say, as usual, that . . ." We often attribute to another, quite without realizing it, our own moods, desires or fears. On the other hand, *healthy* projection lets us understand the other person, predict his behavior . . . which nourishes the relationship: "This is what I've chosen to give him, I think he'll like it."

- **Retroflection** is "holding back" one's feelings or urges, such as desire or anger. I submit to the situation, I "clench my teeth" . . . and in the end I "somatize" such vexations: one day it will be stomach cramps, an ulcer, or even cancer[3]. According to Professor Laborit, most illnesses are linked to such "inhibition of action"—which leads to a build-up of toxic stress hormones in the organism. However, it is also obvious that retroflection is often an appropriate, necessary response; holding back the anger against my boss is more useful rather than dangerous, just as not shoplifting or accosting charming passers-by's are healthy retroflections, which acknowledge that each person has his rightful place, and thereby contribute to social functioning.

- **Deflection** is an avoidance, a deviation of my wants or needs. I "retroflect" my anger against my boss and when I get home, I "deflect" it with speeding or shouting at the children with no good reason . . . If asked an embarrassing question, I "deflect" with a joke, or with general conversation, to avoid answering. Once more, however, deflection can also be useful to avoid unnecessary conflict: I can chat away about something else, or "suddenly remember" an urgent telephone call, to skirt around a delicate issue—that I would prefer to disregard or return to later, under better conditions.

These "resistance" mechanisms are very common, as we have seen, and are unconscious most of the time. Each of us regularly uses several, but not necessarily all of them, and not always for the better. Gestalt Therapy helps me to *identify* and use them in a more appropriate way, and thus *refine contact* rather than interrupt or parasite it. And so, for instance, my *confluence* allows me to adopt a

New York accent in the Big Apple, to be the last to leave when invited to dine with friends (and help them tidy up); my *projections* encourage me to write this book, as I imagine what you, reader, are thinking or feeling; my *deflections* help me keep my good mood and my "joie de vivre" . . . even after the evening TV news!

To illustrate this chapter on resistances, here is a *diagram*, which shows these "boundary events" between the other person and myself:

Resistances in Gestalt Therapy

Some authors distinguish several other "resistances" such as *proflection, egotism, invalidation (devalorisation),* etc.

The *Theory of the Self* will thus help me to clarify my own ways of functioning, mentally and socially, to identify my own contact disturbances, to "clear up" and rid myself of unconscious, *out-dated* habits, to continually readjust my own self-image (e.g.: I thought—from my student years—that "I didn't know how to write," and I said it over and over! In fact, I now see that it is no longer true). All this will allow me to fully utilize all the promise of my latent potential.

Notes

1. The reference book *La Gestalt, une thérapie du contact* (1987; 7th ed. 2003) by Serge & Anne Ginger may be consulted in French, German, Spanish, Italian, Russian, Portuguese.

2. From the Greek *theoreo*: observe, examine, contemplate ("theatre"), and *teoria*: to see (a procession), to examine, theoretical speculation.
3. Recent studies have shown that many illnesses, including cancer, occur more frequently in people who exert exessive control over their anger, sadness or joy (this makes the immune system more fragile).

CHAPTER FIVE

Gestalt-Pedagogy and Socio-Gestalt

Gestalt Therapy in daily life

Up to now, we have concentrated on the *therapeutic* aspects of Gestalt. In fact, historically, Gestalt Therapy stems from an attempt to revise psychoanalysis, and the first American Gestaltists (Fritz and Laura Perls, Paul Goodman, Jim Simkin, Isadore From, Erv and Miriam Polster, Joseph Zinker, etc.) mainly used Gestalt in *individual* therapeutic settings (one or more face-to-face sessions each week, lasting about an hour). The first *groups* were didactic groups, used for *demonstrations or training*. It was only later, in the 60s, that workshops and regular groups became widespread, followed still later by Gestalt interventions in educational, social and medical *institutions, businesses*, and even in *communities* (Gestalt-kibbutz).

Today, non-therapeutic Gestalt interventions have multiplied, in the USA, Germany, Russia, France and elsewhere. For instance: private schools, rehabilitation institutions for maladjusted children, pediatric and psychiatric hospitals, prisons, the Army, drug-dependency units, social services for the abused, for couples or families in difficulty. Also: adult training in areas like commerce, insurance, banks, the media, politics, show business, transportation, industry (auto, chemistry, computing, etc.)

- *Human sciences* have penetrated and become accepted in all sectors. This helps to facilitate contact and communication, manage conflict, stimulate motivation, cooperation, creativity and innovation; at all levels of hierarchy (managers, professionals, employees and workers). Many methods have contributed to this phenomenon:

- *Transactional Analysis* (TA) offers simple, easy ways to understand language, and sheds light on the unconscious "scenarios" and "games" that go on in relationships, as well as the need for social recognition ("strokes") and the individual levels of personal involvement of each person.
- *Neuro-Linguistic Programming* (NLP), which aims for "excellence in communication," stresses for instance the different exchange channels (visual, auditory, kinesthetic, olfactory— more or less dominant in each individual) in our spontaneous "strategies," the importance of unconscious linguistic connotations; it offers techniques to "anchor" the experience, and "reframe" behavior to identify hidden benefits, etc.

What *specificity* does Gestalt Therapy have to offer? There are many, including a renewed art of *contact*, via the use of different phases of the *need-satisfaction* cycle, the unification of the individual's opposite sides (his *"polarities"*) and an increased consciousness of their interdependence. Gestalt helps people achieve their *creative potential*, and find their own personal, original style, in a permanent *creative adjustment* with their environment, as well as rehabilitating the emotional, intuitive and artistic "right brain."

Whilst TA and NLP place importance upon *adaptation* to the other, to the environment and to structures, Gestalt Therapy shifts the balance back towards the *individual*, with his own needs and personal, specific values—which ought not be sacrificed to the permanent pressure exerted by the environment. Gestalt seeks a compromise which takes into account *the situation as a whole*, the "field" of the unique, present experience, "here and now," to find a new, original solution—if possible with a feeling of gratifying *pleasure*, rather than with effort or constraint. Every psychologist and pedagogue knows in fact that the learning experience, within a pleasurable context, is quite different from the experience of systematic learning aimed at better performance. Learning with pleasure is not only more enjoyable but is also *more efficient*. This is, by the way, exactly how we naturally learn to walk, talk and love . . .

Gestalt Therapy thus has a wider scope than just psychotherapy, in the usual sense; it is much more than a "treatment" method. Gestalt brings us a new vision of the world and of relationships, the harmonious development of the personal resources of each person, a full, creative and interactive "life-style," *a new art of living in enriched contact*: this is everyday Gestalt.

Some fields of application

Gestalt—similar to psychoanalysis, in fact—has thus found, over the years, many applications—some of which were unpredictable at the outset. It can accompany us *throughout the ups and downs* of our life, in the most diverse situations: and thus, in parallel with groups available to all (which allow us to enrich our knowledge of the underlying functioning of men and women), we now also see:

- Gestalt groups to prepare for giving birth,
- Special groups for children or adolescents,
- Seminars dealing with sexuality ("Sexo-Gestalt"),
- Others especially for people living alone, for women, for men, for homosexuals, for older people ("Gcronto-Geslalt"),
- Support with illness and preparation for death (especially with cancer, and AIDS). Today, many funeral homes offer support for mourning families.

Gestalt is certainly indicated for people in *difficulty*: illness or neurosis (anxiety, phobias, obsessions, depression, suicidal tendencies, hysteria, etc.), and for mentally ill people (borderline states, or psychosis). It is also just as useful with *normal* people, who face the usual existential difficulties: separation, bereavement, conflict, unemployment, fatigue, agitation, dispersion, immigration, solitude, spiritual crisis, etc. In fact, Perls himself declared that his method was too good to be restricted to the ill.

And thus, today in the USA and in many other countries, most of the hundreds of thousands of people who have had individual "therapy" with Gestalt are not "mentally ill," but are normal people, like you and me, who are keen to enrich their *quality of life*: not only personally, but also professionally and socially. For these same reasons, Gestalt Therapy has been progressively introduced not only into hospitals and institutions for troubled children and adolescents, but also in primary and secondary schools, in adult education institutes (engineers, salesmen, managers, trainers, consultants, teachers of children with special needs, marital guidance counselors, protestant ministers, etc.). Recently, Gestalt has integrated industrial and commercial business: banks, insurance, mass marketing, computer services, chemical factories and metallurgy.

A typical example is that of the *French National Subway corporation* (RATP), which employs 38,000 people, and decided to train the Paris Metro workers in the fundamental principles of Gestalt, following the theme "coming into contact"—in order to improve public reception in stations. Each employee participated in two theoretical and practical training courses, lasting five days (with a series of exercises and "role-playing" games). These courses were centered on the *contact cycle* and its interruptions (avoidances), on verbal and non-verbal communication, behavioral polarities, etc.

The *Ecole Parisienne de Gestalt* (EPG, the Paris School of Gestalt) responsible for this program, began by training the entire personnel of one metro line (260 agents) as well as the management staff and a team of metro trainers—a team that would be responsible for continuing the training of the personnel of the other metro lines, under the supervision of the EPG. Comparable training programs have gone on in other large transport companies (train, bus), including courses aimed at managing professional stress.

Similarly, some specialists of our team have been asked to intervene as experts in several large supermarket chains, in radio and television, in banks—national and foreign (Lebanon), and in the Government (the Environmental Ministry, in France and in Brazil), etc.

The world economic crisis has increased executives' awareness of the increasing importance of "human resources": financial and technological investments are no longer sufficient. The *human* dimension is essential. The underlying motivation of the personnel is what "makes the difference": work completed with enjoyment, a feeling of belonging, of participating in research and creativity, the conviction that each person has his rightful place, that he "matters" to the organization, that he has the right to affirm himself in his difference and his specificity, and *assert himself.*

Gestalt facilitates movement, in executives as much as in professional managers and employees, towards ideas based on *experience* such as mutual respect of individual potential, rhythm, exchange and contact. It highlights the possibility of *positively utilizing certain conflicts*, rather than lamenting them or fighting in vain (thus considering aggression as a "life force," so dear to Perls); it stresses the importance of *informal* relationships, a vital source in the enterprise; it insists on the necessity of including the *ideological* dimension, which cements the organization's culture. Competence is not enough: you have to "believe in it"! Gestalt emphasizes *evolution and change*, and opposes the temptation to maintain a precarious static equilibrium. It offers permanent widening of a whole spectrum of possibilities, via concrete *experimentation* (right brain), and not only based on theoretical laboratory research (left brain).

Gestalt interventions in organizations may take diverse forms. There are many possible presentations, and a variety of "tools": from one-off seminars to initiate managerial staff—including personal involvement exercises and innovation training (using the *Ginger's Pentagram* and role-playing games), regular training sessions with personnel in different levels of hierarchy (working on the contact cycle and its interruptions), individual coaching for managers (using autoscopy[1] in "video-Gestalt"), etc. As always in Gestalt, each program is specific, designed in collaboration with the decision makers according to their real, "here and now" needs, in the social, economic, competitive and cultural context at the time.

To illustrate organizational interventions, here is a quote from a feedback report of one of the trainers of the Paris metro personnel: (*Gestalt and the French Subway Corporation*, RATP):

> I had already heard about *awareness and contact*. Another important notion in Gestalt is that of fluidity, of the "*shuttle*," the back-and-forth nature of interaction. This "shuttle" operates between an "I" and a "thou," between the mind and the body, between the present, past and future. Curiously, there is a similarity inside our company—which symbolizes the shuttle: going from family to work, or vice versa. There are also the ideas of *surface and beneath* the surface. Entering the metro from the surface (the city), going below (the tunnel)—and using Gestalt, to go from what is expressed on the surface, to the problems beneath. (Th. Bonnefoy).

Socio-Gestalt

That which I propose to entitle *socio-Gestalt* (Ginger, 1987) is not the application of Gestalt *within* an organization, but its transposition into an organization (school, hospital, government administration) or a company—globally considered as a "living" organism, in constant interaction with its environment. It is thus a question of extrapolating the usual principles of Gestalt to this metaphor, of the organization as an organism. It is not a Gestalt intervention *in* the company, but rather describes the Gestalt approach *of* the company. Most of the ideas already presented in the *theory of the self* are present here as well.

Notably: all that concerns "**boundary phenomena**" or "resistances". Thus for instance, an organization may suffer from out-dated *introjections* ("cheapest products sell best"; "the clients will get used to it"; "it is better to avoid taking a loan"; etc.) or excessive *retroflection* (budget and results are kept secret, limitation of their own advertising, etc.) and so on.

The balance of all the **functions of the Self** of the organization cannot be maintained if the *decisions* ("ego" function) do not clearly stem from the needs expressed by the personnel and the consumers ("id" function) and upon the company's *identity*: "In our company, we don't do that" ("personality" function or "sacred cows"). A typical example of appropriate action is when *Perrier* courageously decided to recall many millions of bottles of mineral water all over the world, following a temporary error in fabrication. In this way, Perrier respected the consumer's need for security, and the product's image was maintained, which allowed the expense (which acted to promoted the company) to be rapidly written off.

The five poles of the **Pentagram** (Ginger, 1983)[2] need to be transposed and expressed by balanced development of the following:

1. *Material conditions*: offices, equipment, budget, investments . . .
2. *The atmosphere of relationships* in the organization: general ambiance, coffee and lunch breaks, rest rooms, notice boards, social activities, etc.
3. *Technical abilities*: including the quality of products and services, studies and on-going research, availability of technical documents, computers.

4. *The social organization* of the company—both *internal* (struc-
    tures, and role repartition) and *external* (clients and com-
    petition); for instance: charts or "organigrams" showing
    hierarchical distribution of the personnel ("each person has
    his place", and clearly defined relationships), fruitful exchange
    with clients (reception, advertising, needs surveys, etc.).

It is important to note the balance between the two *relationship*
"arms" of the *Pentagram*: which are important not only to ensure that
the internal social *climate* is pleasant, and that each comes more or
less happily to work there, that he feels "at home," and can find
colleagues with whom he can freely exchange; and are also equally
important to maintain efficient internal *structure*: flexible, but clear.
Some companies err on the side of rigor (everything is organized,
but no one can relax), others are too lax (it's "nice" . . . but there is
more chatting than working going on!).

5. *The ideological pole*: the fundamental principles of the
    organization, its "product image," "logo" or motto. These
    demarcate the company from its competitors: originality,
    innovation, reliability, after-sales service, personal attention,
    etc. Often, it is a question of a delicate, somewhat neglected
    aspect, which influences the client considerably—but usually
    unconsciously.

In general, it is easy to transpose the **Twenty principles of Gestalt—**
which I described—to every social organization. We will address
some other examples in Chapter 11.

And thus, the "Gestalt approach" will certainly continue to
develop, in a *wide range of fields*: teaching, training, education, health
and social services, business, far beyond its (more or less) therapeutic
origins.

Notes

1. Observing oneself on the television, in real time, in order to refine one's
    presentation and contact.
2. *See Chapter 1.*

CHAPTER SIX

Gestalt and the Brain

Is Gestalt Therapy "Chemotherapy" Without Knowing it?

As we have seen, Gestalt is used in more and more diverse areas and hardly anyone doubts its effectiveness. But how does it work? How can people really change, *profoundly, rapidly and for a lasting period?* For a long time, we were only able to *observe* that change in attitude and behavior—sometimes surprisingly spectacular—had occurred, without being able to explain how.

Recent neuroscientific research has brought us better understanding of current cerebral phenomena: in fact, every learning experience and every psychotherapeutic intervention acts directly on cerebral circuitry. Internal brain *biochemistry* is modified, as is the production of hormones and *neurotransmitters* (dopamine, serotonin, adrenaline, testosterone, etc.). This is particularly true for those psychotherapies which implicate body and emotions—such as Gestalt Therapy.

Even in recent years, *chemotherapy* (drug treatment) and *psychotherapy* were considered at *opposite* ends of the spectrum. Traditional psychiatrists smiled condescendingly at what psychoanalysts and psychotherapists said; they considered such methods as mere "fashionable worldly entertainment", and they trusted only scientifically tested medication.

After the antibiotic revolution in infectious diseases, there followed the *neuroleptic revolution* in mental illness. At last, there was a whole series of molecules to be developed, which could act directly on the brain and alter behavior (tranquilizers, antidepressants, stimulants, antipsychotics, etc.). In 1952, Henri Laborit introduced a new *psychotropic* (drug acting on the psyche), *Chlorpromazine (Largactil)*, which led to progressive suppression of strait-jackets in psychiatric hospitals. This type of drug became known, in a somewhat exaggerated way, as a "chemical strait-jacket".

Since this time, tranquilizers have become extremely common, and in some countries, like France, Temesta and Prozac are more or less considered "psychological aspirin". These new medicines, although extremely efficient, do have side effects (including sleepiness, loss of initiative, forgetfulness, diminished libido . . . even suicide—if treatment is suddenly discontinued, etc.).

Subsequent practice evolved from the *opposition* to the *association* of drug treatment and psychotherapy. Psychotherapy empowers medical treatment in several ways: it *prolongs and widens* the effects of such medication, which allows progressively reduced dosages. Similarly, drug treatment may help *prepare* the patient for psychological treatment, by reducing anxiety or preventing psychosis.

At present we are entering a third phase: neither *opposition*, nor simple *complementarity*, but *identity* of *a single process with two sides;* we are realizing that, after all, some psychotherapies are in fact a form of chemotherapy. Neurophysiological and biochemical modifications occur with psychotherapy: such effects are rapid and lasting (the pump has been re-primed). This has the major advantage that such internal alterations are *individualized*, with *dosage* adjusted appropriately for the organism, down to the thousand-millionth of a milligram, just as our bodies constantly monitor blood sugar levels, or iron or zinc (without which we would have no sense of smell), or vitamins . . . (To illustrate the importance of micro-dosage, an injection of a *thousand-millionth of a gram* of oxytocin—a hormone which causes lactation, amongst other effects—is enough to provoke an *immediate* reaction of maternal behavior in virgin female rats and ewes.)

It is not possible for an external medication to be as precisely dosed to the *permanent, subtle* variations in individual hormone levels. Each meal and each emotion, affects the balance: just as passing a test can instantly double the blood testosterone[1], and orgasm quadruples endorphin[2] levels! Moreover, two successive blood tests, before and after five minutes of positive visualization, shows a 53% increase in the immune system!

What happens, then, during a Gestalt Therapy session, with body enactment and emotional implication?

The Peak of Evolution

In this chapter, we will briefly investigate *"the most complex structure in the Universe"* (Hubert Reeves), the peak of evolution since the *Big Bang*: the human brain. We will describe in simple terms—illustrated with metaphors—the most recent discoveries of what has been called the "brain decade" (1980—1990), and on the way, see how Gestalt uses them.

If we wanted to summarize the definition of Gestalt, we could say it is a "right brain therapy", which rehabilitates intuitive and synthetic functions as well as non-verbal language (facial and bodily expression, artistic expression).

We could also speak of a "limbic therapy", which could occupy its rightful place with the six fundamental emotions: joy and sadness, anger and affection, desire and fear. Remember that the complex structures of the limbic system are responsible for memory as well as emotion:

> *An experience cannot be memorized unless a sufficient emotional state is induced.*

Similarly a photocopier needs to be warmed up before it works. We learn far better when feeling pleasure, desire or fear that when we feel indifferent, and the Gestalt strategy aims to stimulate a deep emotional response in the client, so that the work that is done is "engrammed" (recorded) permanently, because of modifications (creation of a form, *"gestaltung"*) of the molecular structure. Before continuing with more specific examples of reciprocal interaction between Gestalt Therapy and the brain, here's a brief outline in neurophysiology.

The Neuron

The neuron is the basic nerve cell. It has three main parts:

- A cell *body*, with *nucleus* (containing our genetic inheritance) and the *cytoplasm*—surrounded by a *membrane*, a "contact boundary", essential between the cell and its environment;

- An *axon*, which transmits the message or *nerve impulse*, and can be up to one meter long,
- *Dendrites* (which receive messages from other neurons). One neuron can be in direct contact with up to 10,000 others.

The junction between an axon and the dendrites of the next neuron is called the *synapse*: this is where active contact occurs. There are 10 million millions (10^{13}) synapses per cm³ of cortex—i.e. 10^{15} synapses in the brain, and 10^{278300} possible combinations! . . . a number with 2 million zeros, that would be three miles long if written in characters like these. To count the synapses, one per second, it would need a million employees working full time for 100 years!

A *latest-generation* computer with connections like the brain would be bigger that France, Belgium and Switzerland put together . . . and 10 stories high!

Diagram of a Neuron

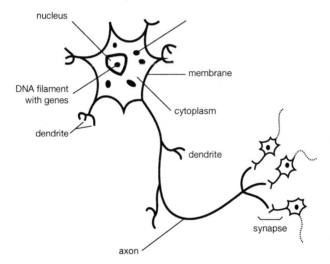

Our brain is thus the most sophisticated "contact machine" of the universe!

All this is so complex and so compact! Just as a basis of comparison, a 5 mm² silicon chip today has a million transistors and can contain the whole of the Oxford dictionary[3]; 230 million HIV viruses could hide under this dot •.

Neurons are built throughout embryonic life, mainly between the 3rd and 7th months *in utero*, at the incredible speed of 300,000 neurons per minute. It is currently estimated that we are born with *100,000 million neurons*; as many as there are stars in the Milky Way. Neurons, unlike other cells, are not renewable[4] (to retain accumulated information), but new branches grow ceaselessly, new connections are always sprouting, according to need (association of ideas and memories, allowing "intelligent" memorization of experiences, and thus learning).

To summarize, the "trees" of our brain are planted from birth, yet the bushes grow and ramify throughout our whole life. This continual *sprouting* is disrupted by alcohol, as well as by some other drugs and prescriptions; it creates *new connections* (such as those created during a Gestalt Therapy session) as well as replacement circuits, when the cells are destroyed by accident or illness.

Contrary to popular belief, *dendritic* growth (which leads to synaptic communication) does not slow down with age . . . It slows down with idleness! Nothing makes us grow old faster than retirement without substitute activities. A baby left alone in the cot without stimulation will not sit until 21 months, and will only walk at three years old! In a hospital room, patients lying near a window with a view to the exterior get better faster. In an "enriched" environment, rats live 50% longer. In general:

"Change and chaos stimulate life".

(Prigogine).

Each neuron is about a thousandth of a millimeter long. If it were as big as a grain of sand, we would need a truck to hold our brain. But don't forget that the neuron is not just a simple grain: it's more like a big town, like Boston—as it consists of hundreds of thousands of macromolecules (or proteins) with different functions, each of which consists of tens of thousands of atoms . . . each of which is made up of tens or hundreds of particles . . . spinning at . . . 4 million km/h (sic)!

In our lifetime, not only most of our neurons fail to renew (in the same way as other cells), but on the contrary at least 100,000 die each day . . . no tragedy, considering that we hardly use 20% of them! The others are like "fallow land", in reserve.

In fact, cellular *death* begins before birth, as 10 to 70% die in fetal life, mostly by cellular suicide (*apoptosis*), to leave more room for the most useful neurons. Indeed, biology is pitiless: all that which is unused dries up and dies fast. Natural selection retains only the essential: *"learning is eliminating"*, as says Jean-Pierre Changeux (1983). At this rate, when we are 80 years old, we still have 70% of our neurons alive—but their repartition is different according to brain area: the *frontal* cortex, where *decisions* are made, have lost 50%—like the *hypothalamus*, regulatory center for hunger, thirst, temperature, aggression and desire . . .

Gestalt therapy particularly stimulates the *hypothalamic* zones (explicit needs in the here-and-now) and the *frontal* lobes (integrative holistic approach, responsibility and decision-making) . . . and thus, it keeps these fragile zones active to *preserve youth and vitality*. Our brains are not like batteries . . . living matter is not tired out with use! Unused, however, neurons oxidize and are literally covered with patches of "rust".

In our 1.4 kg brain, neurons compose barely *250 grams*—which would, by the way, be enough to learn by heart all the books ever printed in the world, since printing was invented (!). Our brain has, in fact, a memory capacity of 125 million million (125×10^{12}) bits of information, i.e. the contents of more that one hundred million books . . . that our brain could theoretically memorize!).

Our organism is astoundingly precise. One example: each cell is surrounded by a *membrane* only 5 millionths of a millimeter thick, with valves that open and close like a vigilant doorman, to specific chemical substances. Each door is variable, and specific to the brain area, and to each instant. All this goes on, evidently, in an "intelligently" coordinated, quasi-instantaneous non conscious way.

Another example. Suppose that someone calls out "Serge", as soon as my ear picks up the *first* letter of my name "S", my synapses have already secreted 3 million active chemical neurotransmitter molecules. It's as if the telephone rang at the same time for each of the 3 million Parisians, alerting them to the possibility of action!

But maybe they answered for nothing! In fact, it wasn't "Serge" . . . but "Simon" who was called! It just goes to show! The post-synaptic membrane regains its resting state within a *millisecond* and is already available for another call. My "gluttonous" enzymes have wasted no time in transforming the erroneously released chemical mediator into an inactive substance. This "contact-withdrawal micro-cycle" will have lasted a mere few thousandths of a second.

Heredity and Freedom

As for the cell's *nucleus*, it harbors all our "past lives", i.e.—more prosaically—the *heredity* of our ancestors, bound up in minute filaments of DNA, grouped in "words" (genes). They have now been decoded and at last we have the detailed map of the 30,000 or so genes in the human genome. When we are born, our "individual program" or "instructions for use" represents a whole library of information, with 3,000 books each with 500 pages, a pile of projects 20 stories high ... to be realized, or not!

Obviously we have certain *predispositions* (height, eye color, hair, health, intelligence, gifted in sport or music, art or contact; and our temperament may be calm or anxious, passive or aggressive, etc.). This genetic code is extremely precise and does not tolerate any "miss-spelling": for one wrong letter, the whole book is discarded (spontaneous abortion).

Thus, as the Orientals are fond of saying, *"all is written"* (not in the heavens, but in the heart of each of my 60 thousand billion cells, from head to toe). The number of possible chromosome combina-tions is so vast that the existence of another Serge just like me is *mathematically impossible* ... from the Big Bang to the end of time (except identical twins, of course). This *irreducible originality of each being* is another theme dear to all Gestalt therapists—who are wary of generalizations regarding "normal" development, and of categorizing mental troubles.

But the fact that "all is written" does not infringe our freedom of choice, as we can *decide to improvise* like an actor, and not follow the text. This deliberate construction of our own future—built from our available heritage—is one of the main goals of all personal and psychotherapeutic development.

"All is written" ... but how shall we read it? We now know that every night we re-read our provisional script, during our *dreams* (Michel Jouvet's hypothesis on "genetic reprogramming"). We re-read and make notes, integrating our own experiences into our species' memory: the secret "book" of our life becomes a "work book", a personal "diary" which facilitates our *individuation*. The

original text of our genetic heritage is thus *readjusted each day,* depending on our experience and the unique events of our existence: this is Gestalt's positive *creative adjustment.*

This work happens partly unconsciously at night, yet *is prepared and is on-going* throughout the day: this is one of the aims of Gestalt therapy, to update our "program" by integrating our experiences into our life project which is freely assumed.

Synapses and neurotransmitters

At each synapse, the electrical nerve impulse is transformed into a *chemical* messenger, via minute vesicles which secrete the *neuro-transmitters*—which emotionally "color" all transmitted information. Almost a hundred neurotransmitters and neuromodulators have been isolated already. For example, every *desire* (hunger, thirst, sex) and every form of *pleasure* (including artistic and intellectual) are correlated to three neurotransmitters:

- *Dopamine,* associated with the tension of *desire;*
- *Noradrenalin,* related to the excitement of *pleasure;*
- *Endorphins,* leading to well-being and *rest.*

Let's recall that *testosterone* is responsible for *aggression* and also *sexual desire*—in women as well as men. These two fundamental *life drives,* survival of the individual and survival of the species are closely linked: they are neighbors in the hypothalamus, separated only by the *pleasure* zone. In Gestalt therapy, we sometimes utilize this "proximity"—for instance, to stimulate weakening sexuality, via playful aggression—easier to manage, with respect for the code of ethics!

These interactions are *circular,* in a feedback loop: and so, vigilance stimulates dopamine production—which in turn maintains or stimulates vigilance. Hunger stimulates eating—which whets the appetite. Success produces testosterone, which stimulates assertive-ness, competition and decision-making—which brings on further success! . . .

Neurotransmitters work in *antagonist pairs* (similar to the classic Gestalt theme of *polarities*). For instance, *dopamine,* the "*awareness, contact and desire hormone*", has a stimulant, tonic effect, which is opposed by the calming, organizing effect of *serotonin*, the "fulfill-ment, organizing, mood-regulating" hormone.

Diagram of vital Hypothalamic functions

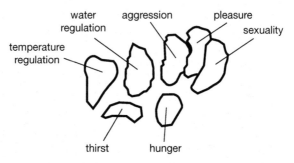

Be aware of the proximity of zones responsible for:
– Aggression, sexuality and pleasure
– Aggression and hunger

Each Gestalt psychotherapeutic action contributes to the *natural* equilibrium of these different internal products. Too much *dopamine* and you have a cerebral "short-circuit": hyperactivity approaching delirium (schizophrenia); not enough, and it's Parkinson's disease, with slowing down and trembling. An excess of *serotonin* leads to obsessive behavior, its lack leads to depression . . .

If you lose control when driving a car, there are two comple-mentary ways to react: slow down the *motor* (reduce dopamine production) or push on the *breaks* (increase serotonin production). The therapist's art is "pushing on the right pedal", deliberately or intuitively, to facilitate a new biochemical equilibrium—which is subsequently auto-regulated by natural secretions.

The "three brains"

Let's put the microscope away, and have a look at macroscopic brain structure. There are three distinct parts to the brain, each one of which includes and *controls* the preceding one.

- The *reptilian brain,* in the heart of the system, is the most primitive part (also present in reptiles). It's a bit like the basement machinery to maintain life: breathing, assimilation, circulation, temperature regulation, etc. This primitive brain is our *instinct* center, formed from birth. It works unconsciously, and remains active throughout sleep and even coma.

- Just above, the *limbic system*—with its many regulatory centers: *emotions*, wakefulness and sleep, desire and aggression. This is where our experiences are recorded, transformed into personal *memory*; this is where the foundations of our personality are built, a synthesis of heredity and daily acquisitions.

This is the target area of choice in Gestalt therapy—which stimulates and explores emotions, combining them in new ways during new experiences, "taming" aggressive and sexual impulses, making them more supple; developing the richness and intensity of all contact.

Diagram of the Brain

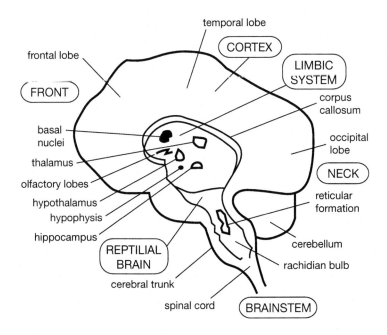

- The two "subcortical" layers in the deep brain are covered by the *cortex*, a thin layer of gray matter in many folds which surrounds and controls everything (unfolded, the cortex would resemble a tablecloth, 63 cm x 200 cm square and 3 mm thick). Sensory information from the *external environment* (sight, hearing, etc.), analyzed by the cortex, is associated with *inner*, often unconscious memories of past experience, as well as with present feelings, from the limbic system.

The whole system is overseen by the *frontal lobes*, which are particularly well-developed in humans, and allow freedom to make an adaptive *decision*. Every *choice* is in fact saying "no" to the rejected solutions. Thus people with frontal lobe damage function virtually automatically: they see a bottle, they drink; they see a bed, they lie down; they see a pretty girl, they approach her: They are very "forward"! They have difficulty resisting temptation, they have little freedom in fact, as they are unable to say "no".

In Gestalt, we regularly stimulate the ability to make conscious choice; at every moment during a therapeutic session, the "client" (= he who is free to ask) is encouraged to make *independent choices and refusals*, and is often provoked into saying "no" (so-called "paradoxical" interventions). Global, "holistic" therapeutic action continually associates the following functions:

- Reptilian (needs);
- Limbic (emotion and memory);
- Corticofrontal (*awareness*, experimentation, decision).

Let us note by the way that Gestalt interventions usually follow the *bio-logical* order (present, past, future) rather than the artificial *chrono-logical* order (past, present, future): we begin with special attention to what is happening in the here-and-now, to 'how" the relation happens (attitudes, postures, tone of voice, sensations, feelings, etc.); then the client may speak about the past, from spontaneously emerging associations; finally, we get to short-term experiments or projects. This is just how ordinary conversations happen:

- You seem tired from the journey . . . would you like a drink? Do you want a cigarette? Make yourself comfortable . . . (*present*).
- What have you been up to, since we last saw each other? Did you get that job? etc. (*recent past*).
- Will you stay for dinner? We could go and see . . . (*near future*).

Here we find the natural structure of our three brains:

- The *reptilian* level manages homeostasis of the *present* (equilibrium of basic needs: temperature, hunger, thirst, etc), as well as survival instincts,
- The *limbic* level is responsible for emotionally charged memories, it integrates conditioned reflexes and learning, from *past* experiences,
- The *cortical* level allows us to choose and make decisions pertaining to the *future*.

Inversely, psychoanalysis encourages the patient to begin with his oldest memories, just as social investigations, medical history (anamnesis), or . . . police inquests attempt to establish the chronological sequence of events by historical reconstruction, *from the past* . . . which is less "present" in our psychological reality!

The two hemispheres

The *right* hemisphere develops before the left, *in utero*. It is the center of global *intuition*, syntheses, the "artistic" brain—which perceives things and situations without analyzing them, or being able to name them. Our culture has over-developed the importance of the left hemisphere, which governs language, logical analysis, science . . . this side is called "dominant". The nerves *cross over*, and thus the left brain controls the right hand—which is why it is seen as dominant!

In reality, our most important decisions are made in the *right* brain (choice of a partner, a religion, a political party, profession, hobby, etc.) and are only rationalized *afterwards* with left brain justification.

Gestalt reacts against this "cultural hemiplegia" by rehabilitating the *right* brain (which is more closely linked, by the way, to the limbic system trough the *perforant path*): faces, bodies, movement in *space*, music, poetry, dreams; *subjective*, phenomenological qualities (*versus objective* quantification), emotions, desires, into the environmental context, with a *circular, systemic* approach—where all the elements are interdependent. The *left* brain manages scientific, mathematical, objective facts, speech, *what* is said rather than *the way* it is said, "the content, not the context", in a Cartesian approach, which is *linear, on a time axis*. This explains why 15% of musicians are left-handed (right brain), compared to only 4% of scientists . . . a difference of 400%.

Therapeutic approaches *engaging bodily and emotional work*—like Gestalt therapy (and rebirth, bioenergy, primal therapy, etc.) associate the *two* hemispheres much more than essentially *verbal* approaches such as psychoanalysis, transactional analysis or neurolinguistic programming, providing that there is plenty of room for subsequent *verbalization*. This usually happens *after* the bodily and emotional movement, whereas in more traditional therapies verbal expression *precedes*—or induces—emotion.

Etymologically, "e-motion" means: movement towards the exterior (*ex-movere*). Emotional "ex-pression" prevents their deeper "im-pression": thus, in working through bereavement it is particularly important to include expression of sadness, so that it does not become lastingly imprinted.

Gender and the Brain

Before ending these few reflections on our two hemispheres, it is important to note a widespread error perpetuated by the non-scientific press: many imagine that the right hemisphere is dominant in *women*, as they are considered to be more emotional. In fact, men get easily carried away, and frequently succumb to passion . . . It is an uncontested fact that *the right hemisphere is more developed in men*—especially due to the effect of the male hormone, *testosterone*.

This explains why, statistically, men are more gifted in general for *spatial* orientation (mechanics, expeditions, . . .) while women have a more developed *left* hemisphere—which facilitates *speech* and *time* orientation.

The most plausible explanation is *evolution*: prehistoric man went off to hunt, silently following the spoor of his prey, while women stayed at home, in the cave, to ensure the rhythms of breast feeding, and family cohesion, via language.

From kindergarten, girls speak four times as much as boys. They have a 12-month lead on boys the same age at 6 years old, and are 18 months in advance at 9. The average length of a telephone call is 20 minutes for (French) women, and only 6 minutes for men. Also, women have developed their senses of hearing and smell: their *hearing* is twice as keen, and six times as many women are pitch perfect! Their sense of *smell* is hundred times as sensitive (even more, at certain moments of the menstrual cycle). Feelings have their own odors: sadness, anger . . . or schizophrenia. We are unconsciously sensitive to a thousand million millionth of a gram of musk, i.e. one single molecule!

Testosterone has many effects: reaction speed, *visual* perception, attention, muscular development, domination instinct, conquest, scarring, etc.: it prepares men for *hunting and fighting.* Men are thus genetically programmed for *competition:* which means that the better man ensures the species' descendance (while women are programmed for *cooperation*).

In parallel, Nature organized male attraction to younger *women*— more likely to childbear. And it also limited mutations in reproducing females, while allowing more "experimentation" in males—of whom more are "not within the norms" (autistics, perverts or . . . geniuses!), which could explain that the great cooks, designers, musicians, poets, etc. are mainly men, independently of cultural conditions— except in the Japanese, whose brain hemispheres work differently.

Psycho-neuro-immunology

Some contemporary Gestaltists do not stop at the recent discoveries concerning central nervous system function and its subtle bio-chemical equilibrium; they are also interested in the largely unexplored domain of *immunology* and its links with the brain.

We have long been aware of the importance of psychological factors in the evolution of many illnesses: following Selye's research, Holmes' and Rahe's studies on stress (1967) revealed to what extent the organism has difficulty adapting to any major event, *positive or negative,* which affects *daily rhythm:* on a scale of *stress* where death of one's partner is rated at 100 points, marriage scores . . . 50 points, losing one's job 47, retirement 45, moving house 20 . . . and holidays 13!

In those people who accumulate 300 stress points within a year, *49% of them develop a serious illness* (cancer, etc.)—compared to only 9% in a control group. Similarly, a British study of 5,000 widowers showed a mortality rate *40% higher* than normal in the year following death of their spouse! Such observations show just how important the psychotherapeutic approach is in the prevention of psychosomatic problems.

Carl and Stephanie Simonton showed the impact of positive *visualization*, as well as mental conviction (*beliefs*) on cancer evolution: 5 years after mastectomy, those who "stoically" bore their illness had 75% metastases and a 38% death rate; whereas in the group who used psychotherapeutic methods (visualization, Gestalt emotional "ex-pression", etc.) these figures dropped to 35% and 10%.

The *placebo effect* is present around 40% of the time. The Birmingham experiment on 400 chemotherapy patients showed that when patients are warned that they will lose their hair, that many of the 30% who took the placebo drug lost theirs too! We also know that the "best" pills are the small red ones!

This confirms the close relationship between the immune system and the brain. There is a lot of exciting research being carried out in this field, at present.

Notes

1. Male hormone, also the hormone of desire, of *conquest* and success; in both men and women.
2. Neurotransmittors of "well-being" and auto-anesthesia.
3. If the automobile industry had progressed as much as computer technology, cars today would weigh 4 pounds, would reach speeds of 600 miles/h, and would cost . . . one dollar!
4. It has been discovered recently that some neurons (especially in the hippocampus) are renewable.

CHAPTER SEVEN

Dreams in Gestalt Therapy

Dreams as "messages"

For Freud, the dream was the "royal gateway" to the unconscious mind. Perls agreed with his master—at least on this point—and even declared that the detailed analysis of a single dream would be sufficient material for a whole therapy!

The book that made Perls famous relates a workshop on dreams, which was tape-recorded. The original title is *Gestalt Therapy Verbatim*—that is *"word for word"* (USA, 1969); whereas the French title is closer to the content: *"Reves et existence en Gestalt-therapie" (Dreams and Existence in Gestalt Therapy)*.

In reality, Perls borrowed his main method of dream analysis from another dissident psychoanalyst, Otto Rank. We will describe a series of complementary approaches to dream work; it does however seem necessary to go briefly over the traditional vision as well as to cover recent research in this area. In fact, although the psycho-analytical approach was dominant from 1900 to 1960, the situation has since evolved, especially since the work of the French researcher Pr Michel Jouvet (Lyon).

Throughout history, dreams have fascinated man, and he has always attempted to decode their messages: 3,000 years ago, prophetic interpretation and therapeutic application of dreams were already practiced in Mesopotamia. In Greece, 420 Esculapian temples were reserved for *incubation*: people slept on the ground, rolled in a bloody animal skin, amongst sacred snakes, and pleaded the gods for dreams, which were supposed to cure their illness . . .!

Remember the Pharaoh's famous dream, of seven thin cows and seven fat cows. Joseph was released from prison, on the grounds of having been able to interpret this dream; he subsequently became Prime Minister of Egypt. We know that in those times, dream interpretation was a highly respected profession. Legend has it that the King's court of Babylon employed 24 well-known onirologists (dream specialists). One day, the King had a dream that he felt was important. Each onirologist offered a *different* interpretation and the King was justifiably puzzled . . . But as it happened, each of the 24 predictions came true, which was a brilliant demonstration of the *polysemic nature* of unconscious language—which takes on many different or parallel meanings (like sacred texts . . . or the Grimm fairy tales!).

The Jews thought of an uninterpreted dream as an unread letter, i.e. as an offence to the author. But, who is the author anyway? Is the dream the expression of the dreamer's unconscious (Freud), or a message from elsewhere?

The collective unconscious (Jung), transpersonal (Grof, Descamps) or divine inspiration—which would explain premonitory dreams?

Or could it simply be a natural, essential biological phenomenon (Jouvet, Dement, Hobson)?

Recent research

Today we know that only the more developed species dream. Cold-blooded animals (fish, reptiles) never dream, but their nervous system self-regenerates throughout their life (permanent *neurogenesis*), renewing neurons just like ordinary cells. And thus, they are reduced to *inborn instincts* and are unable to *learn or acquire conditioned reflexes* . . . they cannot benefit from psychotherapy—unlike cats, dogs, horses . . . and dolphins (who sleep with only one hemisphere active at a time!).

During the dream, the animal is particularly *vulnerable*: it is temporarily deaf and paralyzed. It is not surprising that to be able to dream, a certain *security* is required. Thus, cows dream three times as much in the stables compared to in the fields! And the large carnivores, sure of themselves, let themselves dream up to 40% of their sleeping time, while the less secure prey hardly dare dream more than 5% of their sleep time.

Man himself spends about 20% of his sleep time in dreams. This amounts to around 100 minutes each night—which he may remember or not. Everyone has dreams, but a mere *eight minutes* after waking, 95% of the content is forgotten!

The fetus starts to dream *in utero*, from the 7th month after conception (thus, before it is possible to repress conscious experience, according to Freud hypothesis), and the newborn continues cerebral construction as such during 60% of the time. The pregnant woman has twice the dreams she would normally have, to "accompany" her child's neurogenesis. It is not impossible that some of these dreams allow unconscious transmission of certain life experiences, which would contribute to the famous "heredity of acquired characteristics"—which are not transmitted genetically, by nuclear DNA, but may be transmitted by cytoplasmic mitochondria as well as early recording during "paradoxical sleep" (Ginger, 1987).

The Third state

We are aware today that—just like matter—we have *three states*: wakefulness, sleep and *dreaming*. The latter, still called "paradoxical" sleep, is as different from sleep as from wakefulness and implies significant cerebral activity: 2/3 of the *right* brain is mobilized, in the *hypothalamus* (needs), *limbic area* (emotions and memory), *cortex* (visual images) and *frontal lobes* (synthesis, projects, vision)—while the *left* brain (rational verbal analysis and logical criticism) is reduced to a minimum. However, communication between the two hemispheres, via the *corpus callosum*, continues during dreamless sleep.

Our memories are encoded and *stored during dreaming*, especially those with emotional content, and important experiences, either positive or negative. Memorizing of *complex* processes undertaken during the day goes on mainly during the first hour of sleep. During the dreams, the brain is active, and uses as much glucose as it does when awake, which explains why we lose weight while dreaming.

A dream-deprived rat loses much of its learning ability. The same applies to patients who are on long-term neuroleptic or anti-depressant medication—both of which reduce or abolish dreaming. Prolonged dream deprivation seems to lead to compensatory delirium, which may be either aggressive or sexual[1], as well as bulimic tendencies.

One of the functions of dreams could be the *daily revision of our genetic program,* and its *daily update* following the experiences during the preceding day—the hypothesis of "genetic reprogramming" evoked by Pr Jouvet. Another function could be the maintenance of the *neuronal network,* when damaged circuits are repaired . . . just as each night, the underground train lines are discretely cleaned up and repaired!

Thus dreaming may be responsible for *two opposite and complementary* functions:

- It could represent the "umbilical cord for the species"—which nourishes us with our origins and valorizes the *survival functions* (aggression and sexuality): cats dream about hunting and pouncing, while mice dream about running away! And men dream about . . . sexuality! It is interesting to note that Eskimos dream about *snakes*—although they are non-existent in their climate (this supports the Jungian notion of *archetypes*). Dreaming thus plays a role of "shielding us from our culture"—since our education is usually quite restrictive about the expression of such vital impulses.
- However, dreaming could also be an important factor of *individuation* (that which makes me *different* from my neighbor), as my own unique experience is taken into consideration.

Dreaming could therefore facilitate integration of my own memories into our collective cultural memory, which ensures the essential function of synthesis of both hereditary and acquired characteristics (*nature and nurture*).

If this hypothesis were to be completely confirmed by current research, it would be during paradoxical sleep that our long-term memories would be "engrammed" (engraved) in the cerebral structures. If this is indeed so, then in order to avoid the psychological "scars" of a traumatic event, the short-term memory could be "erased" before becoming fixed in the long-term memory: i.e. *before the next dreams occur.* (A process analogue to that of wiping a displayed computer message, before saving it to the hard disc (Ginger, 1987).

"Gestalt-emergency"

We have successfully tested this personal hypothesis, time and again: an "emergency" psychotherapeutic intervention, *prior to the first night*, helps dedramatize traumatic events such as rape, accident, attack, arson, fire, suicide of a loved one, etc., as it allows deep emotional expression within the *security* of a therapeutic session. The event can be replayed in a *modified* version, where the victim takes on a more *active* role rather than staying in a state of "inhibition of action" (Laborit, 1979). This method seems to diminish the trauma because the immediate "ex-pression" avoids the lasting "im-pression" in deeper brain structures. Victims subsequently recount the painful event less emotionally, with greater distance, as if they were uninvolved witnesses.

Here is an example among many:

A young woman driving down a mountain loses control, her car slides, rolls over several times, and crash-lands 20 meters below the road, in a ravine. The car is wrecked, yet fortunately the driver is thrown free and manages to grab hold of a bush; she is unhurt, but badly shaken by the shock: she thinks she has died! During the therapeutic session—mere hours after the accident—I made her go further than just telling me the story, in a kind of debriefing: she mimed it, enacted her fantasies about death, and cried out her fear and anger—to reduce her internal tension by ex-pressing it externally. Above all, I encouraged her to imagine and role-play different *active* roles: she "became" her car, jumped off the road deliberately, then flew up like a plane, etc.

These games dedramatize the situation and allow her to emerge from her role as *victim, imprisoned* inside the car, deprived of all responsibility.

After an hour of going through all the aspects of the accident, she regained her breath, in a calm mixture of laughter and tears.

The next day, when she accompanied the police to the scene and described what had happened, calmly and precisely, they scarcely believed that she had in fact been at the wheel of the car . . .

We therefore suggest the creation of *emergency psychological services*, an "Emergency Gestalt" network—where people could go, without appointment, the *same day* of the accident or attack, for a cathartic working-through of the experience, before the night, *before the first dreams*[2].

Freud, Jung . . . and the others

Freud considered that "dreams have the power to heal, to relieve suffering," and his follower Ferenczi thought of dreams as "traumatolytic": that they could dissolve trauma, and "digest" it unconsciously. This would particularly apply to repetitive, "recurring" dreams—which seem to progressively reduce the *emotional atmosphere surrounding the memory* of the stressful situation.

For Freud, dreaming is often a "neurotic symptom"; it is not a *transcendent* message from above, but an *immanent message from below*, from the "Dark Continent" of unconscious impulse. Jung elevated the status of dreams, as he considered them not to be just traces of biological or psychological events, but also an unconscious perception of the *common cultural ground* of humanity. For Jung, dreams stretch out unbroken into the past, as well as into the *future*. Dreams do not *hide* repressed desires, but in fact *reveal* material from the *collective unconscious* and can even take on an esoteric meaning.

The following illustrates Perls' approach to dreams:

Each element in the dream represents a different part of the dreamer's personality. As the goal of each one of us is to become healthy and therefore *unified*, we must *assemble the dream fragments*. He went on to state that we must *reintegrate all these projected elements*, which belong to our personality, and thus reveal the hidden potential of the dream. We *do not interpret* dreams in Gestalt therapy. We do something much more interesting: instead of analyzing them to death by performing an autopsy, we *bring them to life*. We do that by bringing the dream into the *present*: instead of relating it as a past event, we can re-enact it in the present so that it becomes part of ourselves. He suggested that if you want to work *alone* on a dream, to write it down, list *each and every* element, omit no detail, and work upon each part of it by *becoming* each element, one by one.

(to paraphrase *Gestalt Therapy Verbatim*.)

Certain Gestalt Therapists, like Isadore From, go further and consider the dream (especially the night preceding or following a session) not only as a projection but also as a *retroflection*, i.e. an important disturbance of the *contact-boundary* between client and therapist. The sleeping person would say to *himself* [3], unconsciously, what he avoids expressing to *his therapist.*

He thought that a client in therapy knows in general that when he remembers a dream, he will tell his therapist. He considered that this fact predetermined, in a way, dream content: it is not just a dream, it is a dream *that he will tell his therapist about.* Isadore From also said that another name for "retroflection" could be "censoring" or "retention": the patient speaks to himself, tells himself things that he could not, or would not want to tell his therapist. I. From thus reintroduces, more or less explicitly, the notion of *transference*, which he describes as the equivalent of the "here and now." He continues by remarking that the point of transference is to facilitate the finishing-off of *unfinished business* from the past, and that while *we do not encourage* transference, as it is practiced in psychoanalysis, we cannot eliminate it. It would be ridiculous to pretend that we do not use transference. We simply ask questions likely to alert the patient to his transference, and reduce it.

10 practical approaches to dreams

We use no less than *ten different therapeutic approaches* to dreams—which when combined can help the work of the client and of the Gestalt Therapist. You could even use one of your own dreams to explore these possibilities, one after another (but if you are alone, number 6 may prove a challenge!).

1.   *Do nothing*: the dream *itself*, independent of any deliberate use, has as we have seen, many *natural* "therapeutic" functions. These include biological adaptation and selfregulation, which do not necessarily require conscious re-memorization: revision and updating of genetic heritage, experience assimilation, behavioral individualization (Jouvet), progressive dissolving of trauma (Ferenczi).

2.   *Recount the dream*: merely recounting the dream upon waking is useful: as the dream is *brought into the consciousness*, spontaneous associations and *dedramatization* can occur.

3. *Interpret the dream:* interpretations via *associations* (with either form or content), and deciphering symbols (Freud) facilitates a rich detour into the individual unconscious.
4. Universal, *collective unconscious* symbolic references, as well as hidden messages regarding the future (Jung) introduce a *transpersonal and spiritual* dimension of potential "revelation."
5. *Play the dream*: the dream may be enacted, as a collective *psychodrama* (Moreno), to bring out certain aspects and enrich the reactions of the various protagonists.
6. *Amplify the key sentences*: the *group* can function as an amplifier; the therapist entrusts certain *key phrases* from the dream to group members—who will speak them aloud at the end of the session (Anne Peyron-Ginger).
7. Enact each part of the dream as a *projection of the dreamer* (Perls): it encourages a reunification of the varied facets of the individual, by step-by-step repossession of seemingly disparate elements.
8. Ask the dreamer *if the dream concerns the therapist*: consider the dream as a *retroflection* (I. From) enriches the exchange and *transference* between therapist and client, which lies at the heart of every psychotherapy, particularly Gestalt.
9. Ask the dreamer *to finish the dream*: the dream may be considered to be an *unfinished Gestalt* (Perls, Ginger, Quattrini): in fact, by its very nature dreaming happens during sleep, and is *unconscious*—just like digestion. When digestion becomes conscious (stomach ache, etc) it means that something is wrong. We can assume that if the dream spontaneously *emerges into consciousness* upon waking, that is has not been completely "digested". In this case (and only in this case[4]), we can be very attentive to *helping the client finish the unfinished business.* For instance, one suggestion could be that the client tells the dream in the present, then ends it *as he chooses:* he is thus *responsible*—as the dream is his own—and he remains *active* as he enacts a monodrama, to reduce the unconscious psychological tension of "unfinished business" and thus builds his own future. For Quattrini, the *emotional flavor upon waking* is more important than visual memories. He considers the dreamers' *confluence* with his emotions.

10. *Forget the dream*: finally, the dream may simply serve as a *pretext* for further exploration, like a *springboard* from which the session begins. The therapist can pay more attention to *how* the dream is told in the *here and now* (tone of voice, breathing rhythm, gestures, posture, relationship with the therapist, etc), than to the dream content—and the therapist can even ignore the dream completely!

As we can see, the Gestalt therapist has many resources to explore this "royal pathway" (Freud). Several approaches may be used in succession, or can be combined in a mutually enriching way[5].

P.S. Most of these approaches can also be applied to working on drawing and painting (*Gestalt Art Therapy*).

Notes

1. We know today that physiological sexual excitation *precedes* every dream (for about 2 minutes), that this occurs at every age, in both genders, and *independently* of dream content (contrary to Freud's hypothesis).
2. Of course, EMDR technique can also help a lot to «reorganize» the memories.
3. *Translator's note:* for simplicity, we have kept the French masculine form to include both genders.
4. I myself do not agree with the idea of mercilessly pursuing every dream, which sometimes resembles "rape of the unconscious" (as if we did not trust it to continue to work all by itself). Neither do I hold with the notion that non-dreamers are somehow"guilty" (they are often suspected of repressing, etc).
5. See the video tape or DVD «*epg@gestalt.asso.fr*» «*Singular Views: Gestalt Therapy in Paris*», EPG, 2000.

CHAPTER EIGHT

The Body, the Emotions

Is Gestalt a body oriented Psychotherapy?

Is Gestalt a "body-oriented" psychotherapy, or, better yet, "therapy *mediated* by bodily and emotional implication"? This is what we hear so often.

In fact, Gestalt therapists are far from agreement on this matter! All Gestalt therapists pay attention to the body and closely observe posture, breathing, eye contact, voice, micro-gestures, etc., but while some use purely *verbal* interaction, others propose that the *client* mobilizes his body, or even engages in physically implicating experiments; still other therapists also use *their own bodies*, and *touch* the client, right up to a sort of "therapeutic body-body".

Fritz Perls himself, having just left psychoanalysis for Gestalt Therapy, began with his patients lying on the couch. Later, he used a face-to-face approach, invited his clients to move about, but rarely did so himself: he was growing older, and rarely left his legendary armchair . . . all the while holding his eternal cigarette in one hand!

As for Laura Perls, she affirms that: *"There is one thing that I cannot stress enough: bodywork is an integral part of Gestalt therapy. Gestalt is a holistic therapy—that is, it takes the whole organism into consideration, not just the voice, the words, the action or whatever else."*

She continues, *"I use all sorts of physical contact if I feel that it can help the client take a step toward his awareness of the present situation (. . .). I have no particular rules concerning male or female patients. I may light a cigarette, feed someone with a spoon, do a girl's hair, hold hands or hold a patient close to my breast, if I think it is the best way to establish non-existent or interrupted communication. I touch the patients, I let them touch me, to experience growth of their body awareness."*

From 1959, she noted that *"There seems to be great divergence of opinion and much anxiety regarding the acceptability of physical contact in therapy."* Indeed, such contact is still often criticized 40 years later, and is even considered "taboo" by many cultures and sub-cultures: in traditional psychoanalysis, in many religions . . . and in many Anglo-Saxon countries!

Proxemics is the study of the symbolic meaning of space in various cultures (Edward Hall, 1971), and of socially correct distance and contact: handshaking, embracing, kissing, etc. This theme of the *optimal distance* at each moment between two people is essential in Gestalt, as it affects the quality of contact.

Laura Perls does not separate Gestalt Therapy from artistic and bodily expression. She herself was trained in music, dance and diverse body techniques (Alexander, Feldenkrais, Steiner, etc.) whilst simultaneously continuing psychoanalytical training.

However, some well-known Gestalt therapists rarely use the body *actively* or *interactively*: they prefer instead to observe or interact *verbally*, without involving their own bodies. This seems something of a paradox, to encourage the client toward total, unified expression of his being, while remaining firmly within purely verbal expression!

Of course, the fundamental theory and methodology specific to Gestalt Therapy does not mean *obligatory* bodily mobilization: the global phenomenological approach, the *Theory of the Self, awareness* of current processes in the here-and-now of the relationship, identifying disturbances in the contact cycle, and resistances, etc., all of that hardly requires active physical intervention. However, it seems to me that this *limits* therapeutic possibilities which could otherwise contribute to the intensity and depth of therapeutic work, increase efficiency, and decrease the duration of therapy.

- Most current Gestalt practitioners place *great importance on the physical experience* of the client—as well as that of the therapist. They are as much interested in *sensory receptivity* ("What do you feel now?") as *motor activity* of the organism ("I invite you to stand up and take a few steps . . . ") and they do not hesitate to move about *themselves* (modifying, depending on the situation, the physical distance, or engaging in physical contact—even "therapeutic tenderness" or physical confrontation). It is not just a question of *speaking about* the body, but of speaking *with* the body, *through* the body, from "body to body"—just as we can speak "from heart to heart." Of course, such close proximity requires mutual trust and a *strict code of ethics*. In practice, it remains the exception in *individual* therapy—where there is a greater risk of ambiguity; however it is much more common in a *group situation*.

"Games" or "Exercises"

When Gestalt Therapy was growing most rapidly in California (1964–1974), several *non verbal exercises* to enhance contact were created:

- Moving around the room with all senses active (looking, touching, smelling, etc.),
- Finding one's "right place" in the room;
- Meeting a partner, eyes closed, or back-to-back,
- Physically defending one's "territory,"
- Testing confidence, by letting oneself fall into the group's arms,
- Or exploring one's mistrust, by staying all alone . . .

Such warm-up exercises may reduce certain cultural inhibitions; they may concern the *group as a whole*, or a particular *client*, and can have various experiential objectives, leading to insight: feelings of abandonment, letting go, affection, being closed-in, confrontation, risk, discovery, confidence, limits, etc.; they lead to discovery of new facets of oneself; they also can make implicit situations *explicit*, through enactment or *amplification*.

However, wrongly used, with a lack of regard for actual preoccupations in the here-and-now, they risk **inducing** an *externally provoked* emotional or relational situation that does not obviously correspond with the actual personal feeling of each participant. And so, today, such "games" are usually only proposed occasionally, the priority is for whatever emerges *spontaneously* in the here-and-now of the client's experience (there is a tendency to work with one *individual* client, whether in the group or dual setting).

In the *dual* setting, direct physical interaction between therapist and client is more limited, and more delicate to manage, for several reasons:

- *Material*: lack of partners;
- *Psychological*: transferential feelings can get in the way (the therapist could unconsciously represent a parental image, a romantic or professional partner, etc.);
- *Deontological*: risk of ambiguous sexual connotation in expression of tenderness and caring, as well as limitation in expression of "aggressive" confrontation.

On the other hand, in the *group* setting, such contact can generally be explored in security, and even amplified, and in any case, with much commentary:

- "What do you feel when you lean against me?"
- "What happens when you feel suffocated like that?"
- "I always dreamt of sitting on my father's knees," etc.

However it may happen, such "exercises" or "dramatizations" are rarely *preprogrammed* (except—as noted above—as warming-up sequences for a workshop).

The misunderstanding would be to *alternate sequences* of body and verbal exchange, during a workshop: it is rather suggested to work on *every level at once*: physical, emotional, intellectual, social and spiritual. Proceeding otherwise would be contrary to the spirit of Gestalt—which offers a *global*, holistic approach to the human being in the situation of a given field—while taking into consideration the five principal dimensions of man and their continuous interactions.[1]

Body awareness

In fact, the Gestalt practitioner prefers to draw on, at each moment, and with constant *awareness*, that which emerges spontaneously, "as it happens, and when it happens". He is particularly attentive to all of the physical manifestations of his client: posture and movement, as well as semi-automatic *micro-gestures*, like "Freudian slips *of the body*" which reveal processes that are mostly unconscious. For instance, tapping fingers, rocking feet, mini-contractions of jaw muscles. Of course, he also surveys the tone of voice, the *breathing* rhythm, and the blood *circulation*—especially noticeable at the carotids (neck arteries) or via turning pale or blushing. He does not lose sight of the fact that the body can convey at the same time *personal expression* (I feel tired) and language, or *interpersonal communication* (this is how I can show you that I am tired).

As I already remarked in the first chapter, in Gestalt, the *physical symptom*, occasional or chronic (such as a feeling of oppression, migraines, tenacious back ache), is readily used as an "entrance", which allows direct contact with the client; an entrance which frequently respects (unconsciously) the path that he has himself "chosen".

We would encourage the client to be attentive to what he is feeling: this is the global realization or "*awareness*". We would suggest to him to maybe *amplify* his feeling or *symptom*—in order to better observe it, like through a magnifying glass, and to let it "speak"— which is an attitude specific to Gestalt, as the traditional medical approach aims to *attenuate* symptoms: in fact, if the body attracts our attention and we do not listen, it tends to "cry out" louder and louder! Psychotherapy does not try to "cover up," but to "dis-cover."

Don't feed the symptoms

The Gestalt Therapist does not try to immediately "decode" the symptom at any price—which would sometimes become "feeding the symptom with meaning," according to the famous psychoanalyst Lacan. In fact, and contrary to widespread popular opinion, the *understanding*—even exact—of the origin or meaning of a psychological symptom does not always help promote healing; on the contrary, it can even contribute to *maintaining it, by justifying it.*

For instance, saying: "If I am aggressive and violent, it's because I identify with my father," or "If I am impotent, it's because my overprotective mother always "castrated" me and forbade any initiative," can imply deterministic submission: "Since I have plenty of excuses to be aggressive or impotent, my childhood being what it was, it's completely *natural* that I am like this," or even: "With such a past, I am condemned to stay like this!"

The body can lie too

The Gestalt practitioner is careful about making any *interpretation* of gesture or "body language" according to a *pre-established* code, which is the technique proposed by Alexander Lowen in his bioenergetic approach. One of Lowen's principles, "the body never lies!" is often heard. However, it is obvious that the body takes liberties: I can feel terrific because I've drunk alcohol; a mere toothache can cause great suffering, whereas cancers can grow silently; I can have an erection despite myself, or my penis could disappoint me when anxious, confronted by a too-strong desire . . . In reality, we can blindly trust neither body nor words!

Rather than trying to *interpret* the behavior of another, the Gestalt therapist prefers to encourage the client *himself* to pursue the exploratory path that presents itself spontaneously. Thus by successive association of feelings, gestures, images, sounds or words, sudden *insight* to current behavior, or to unconscious, archaic, stereotypical behavior, often occurs.

The therapist is *active and interactive,* but is not "directive." He invites, for instance, *amplification* of observed phenomena, or even *experiments* with new attitudes (chosen by the client). The therapist may *react,* but he does not fix the *direction* of the action.

The therapist's own body

The Gestalt therapist intervenes *verbally,* and also with *silence.* He intervenes with his posture, his attitudes, and his *immobility*—as much as with his deliberate movements and gestures.

"Whatever you do, you cannot *not* communicate!"
(Palo Alto School).

This said, the therapist himself is incarnated . . . and just as well! His own body will help him to actively accompany his client, with *controlled involvement.* His spontaneous physical sensations will act as a "compass" to guide him through the maze of relation. If he feels tense, on edge, worried, bored or irritated, or on the contrary, moved, touched, seduced . . . far from wanting to artificially neutralize these feelings, the Gestalt therapist will consider them in part as pre-conscious responses to the attitude and discourse of the client, and the awareness of his *counter-transference* as well as of diverse *resonance* phenomena, will enrich his understanding of what happens.

He will frequently share with his client ("I don't know why, but I feel more and more bored while I listen to you ..." or: "I feel oppressed ... ") or even, he will express it with an action (approaching, getting up, moving away, etc.), in order to incite insight.

Sometimes, he will deliberately use his body to underline, amplify or deepen a particular situation and he will propose an *incarnated* therapeutic exchange—especially in a *group* setting (to avoid misunderstanding, and respect an irreproachable deontological position). This could be: taking someone in his arms and letting him cry there, or just the opposite, provoking the client by holding him firmly or by pushing him—to release a healthy defense reaction ("paradoxical" therapy).

Therapeutic "body-body"

Close physical contact in therapeutic "body-body" often allows feelings that are deep, forgotten, denied or suppressed to emerge: such as inexpressible rage that has led to guilt, following premature "abandonment" by the client's mother when she died from illness. Sometimes, even more archaic[2] emotions are experienced, going back to a pre-verbal period (the "bad taste" of a rejecting mother's milk, even nostalgia of the well-being in the "oceanic" intra-uterine period). This type of experience is not rare during specific Gestalt work in a pool warmed to body temperature.

We all know that the senses of smell and taste are already developed *in utero*. *Haptonomy* (Frans Veldman), with its practice of fetal caressing through the abdominal wall, confirms the precocious nature of cutaneous sensitivity. The sense of *touch* is that which occupies the greatest body surface, as well as mobilizing by far the most nerve endings. Whereas we can live deaf or blind, it is not possible to survive if over one seventh of the skin is destroyed. Freud and the psychoanalysts are particularly interested in *three of the orifices* of the human body (mouth, anus and genitals), whereas Perls and the Gestalt Therapists work with the millions of pores all over the skin! Köhler's famous experiments with baby monkeys showed that the babies sought *skin contact* and bodily *warmth* from their mother more than her milk. In general, it is clear that *tenderness* is fundamental nourishment, sadly "censored" by our culture.

Speaking of bodywork, it is interesting to note that, contrary to popular opinion, certain therapeutic physical interventions are *less inducive* for the client than verbal interventions, and are therefore less alienating and more respectful of the client's autonomy: in fact, he remains free to "read in" to the intervention what he likes—which allows him the liberty to reply or not, as suits him, as these interventions are often less explicit, and are *polysemic* (bearing multiple meanings). The *client himself* finds his own meaning.

And so, to give a simple example, if *as a therapist, I move back a step* at a particular moment, the client may:

- move forwards to maintain the same distance,
- he may on the contrary move back himself, to imitate the therapist,
- he may feel "abandoned,"
- he may feel more freedom, and rejoice in the sensation of more space,
- he may not react at all, or even not notice . . . or pretend to not notice,
  . . . And so on . . .

In other words, he is *free to react as he likes* to the situation I created. I am obviously not "neutral," and I acted the way I did:

- either intuitively (given my counter-transference of the moment),
- either as part of a plan, a deliberate therapeutic strategy.

However, whatever the situation, the *polysemic* nature of reading the physical reaction allows the client his own *creative adjustment*, which is his own *responsibility*. This occurs much more readily than if I said to him for instance: "Well, when you do that, I just want to move away!"

From body to words; From words to body

When a gesture or posture is amplified, insight can be progressively approached: this is the classic pathway from *physical to verbal expression*.

Here is an example:

During a session, Helen fiddles with her neck chain while speaking. I point this out to her and suggest that she continues, and amplifies what she is doing . . . It soon leads to tears: it brings back the memory of her son, who died of an accident, many years ago at age 5, while she was out with her lover. Since then, she has unconsciously been "chained up" and can feel no pleasure, to pay for her "crime." After several sessions, she can resign herself to the idea of taking off the chain and put it away in a case—free of guilt. Feeling free at last, she can finally lead a satisfactory life with her partner.

But in Gestalt, we also work the other way around, i.e. *from words to body*—especially with techniques such as deliberate *enactment*, inspired by psychodrama:

The client (C): I have no future in my work, but I don't dare leave. All the reasons to stay or to leave go *around and around* in my head, with no result . . .

The therapist (T): get up and turn around and around, here in the room! . . . What do you feel?

He gets up and walks around in the room, in front of the group who are seated on cushions on the floor.

(C): It annoys me! It won't lead to anything! I'm just going around and around! I want to find a way out!

(T): Well, try to get out!

(C): Here, there's only one way out: by the door!

(T): Well, go out the door then! What are you waiting for?

(C): I can't get past! There's a woman sitting in the way!

(T): Speak to her.

(C): Why are you stopping me leaving? What are doing, looking at me like that? . . . You fascinate me! . . . I could go around you and leave anyway . . . but I don't want to: I like you! I would rather stay and chat with you . . .

(T): Is there anyone else you could say that to?

(C): Ummm . . . Yes! My work colleague!

(T): What would you say to her?

(C): I like you! I like seeing you there every day at work: we get on well . . . Deep down, I don't want to leave my department! . . . If I asked for a promotion, I'd have to go to another department. I'd rather stay where I am!

(After a silence) . . . I thought I wasn't ready for more *responsibilities*, but finally, I think that I'm just not ready to *leave you!* But it's silly! There's nothing to stop us having lunch together every day!

In the days that followed, he applied for—and obtained—a promotion to a neighboring department! It was enough to enact the situation—symbolically—to realize that the problem was not where he'd thought, it was elsewhere. The physical movement mobilized his feelings and "unlocked" the associations, allowing him to find a way out of the dead end.

Limbic opening

We have just illustrated a classic sequence that we've already discussed:

abstract verbalization
→ physical mobilization
→ right brain
→ limbic brain
→ emotion
→ memory (associated with emotion)
→ associations
→ insight
→ decision
→ verbalization

For this sequence to begin, the motor needs "warming up." Similarly, starting the process of memorization leading to a lasting imprint of an experience implies "limbic openness" (Ginger, 1987): *movement of the body* in space mobilizes the *right hemisphere* and "opens the door" to emotion and association.

A simple yet spectacular way to see this is to do a drawing in a notebook (a scholarly activity, mobilizing the rational *left* brain), then to do the same drawing, but larger, on a paperboard, standing up in public: just getting up, moving the body, in front of others, mobilizes the *right* brain (spatial, relational, emotional) as well as the limbic brain . . . and the result is quite different, and is accompanied by significant *insight*!

However, *verbalization* remains useful to "entitle" the experience and to be able to *relocate it*; just as one can entitle a document before filing it on the hard disk of a computer, or label drawers where diverse books and materials are kept—to facilitate subsequent location. Otherwise, the physical and emotional experience is merely *recorded*, and is more difficult to find and *use* when necessary. This explains the importance of time for verbal "feedback".

Emotional work unaccompanied by verbal exchange frequently leaves little lasting usable traces—whilst *verbal* work unaccompanied by emotional and physical involvement leaves few deep modifications in the short term, and requires many repetitions. It is only the *combination of the two*—emotion *and* verbalization—which seems to bring about transformation which is *rapid, profound and lasting*.

Psychoanalysis allows the passage from the spoken word to emotion (but not the body in movement), whereas Gestalt therapy especially favors moving from the body to the feelings, and then to the spoken word.

Gestalt Therapy does not encourage us to master or *control* our emotions . . . i.e. reduce them to slavery! But rather to "tame" them, to get to know them better and make friends—with whom we can dialogue in confidence. It is a matter of not fighting *against*, but progressing *with*.

Our emotions are there to help us, and not to handicap us: fear or anger protect us from danger, sadness allows us to work through *mourning* (real or symbolic; death, separation, abandoning a project). In order to "digest" the experience, it is often necessary to "masticate" or chew over it, rather than trying in vain to forget. It is said that the *normal* time to mourn a loved one is four seasons (the first Christmas without him or her, the first holidays . . .). After *two years,* persistent bereavement may be considered "pathological" and may require treatment.

Tears are the emotions' "lubricant": they help feeling to circulate. They may be present not only with sadness, but also joy, pleasure, or admiration. They "clean out" the organism, and evacuate up to 40% of the excess neurotransmitters produced. It is thus unhealthy to forbid crying; and in fact such control disturbs the immune system and creates favorable ground for the development of serious illness, such as cancer—which develops more often in people who never express emotions, considered by society as "negative," such as fear, anger or sadness.

Words are not enough! For them to work, they need to be "felt": we need to embody them.

> To reach Man, *"the Word became flesh"* . . .
> . . . but to be more manageable,
> the flesh is made Word!

Notes

1. See Chapter 1, *Ginger's Pentagram.*
2. Such regressive experiences towards a normal "archaic" nucleus should not be confused with pathological *decompensations* towards a "psychotic nucleus."

Vital Drives: Aggression and Sexuality

A force, or "drive", "urges" us to live, to go forwards. It's our internal "motor", which energizes our daily life, from birth to death. Different psychologists have highlighted the basic importance of one or another of these innate drives. Today, three of them are generally recognized as fundamental: hunger, aggression and sexuality (remember how close their regulating centers are situated in the hypothalamus. *See diagram, chapter 6*).

Hunger

Right from birth, *eating* allows us to select from the external world what we need in order to grow. Perls considered hunger as a primary need and he deliberately extrapolated it beyond *material* nourishment: we also need *affective, intellectual and even spiritual nourishment* throughout our existence; we are careful to take what we need and what we want from our environment. Just as with food, it is a question of *choosing* what is right for us, at each moment, chewing it up and digesting it to make it part of us, and rejecting the excess.

In a healthy organism, this process is unconsciously *autoregulated*: it has been demonstrated that babies as young as 1 year old, when free to choose from a huge *self-service buffet*, after the first few days where they choose according to whim, will spontaneously eat—as do animals—a healthy balanced diet. The "dietary sense" is *genetically programmed*—and succumbs progressively to our artificial and dependent lifestyle.

This theme of active, individualized *assimilation*, rather than passive *introjection* without discernment, is central in Gestalt, as we have already underlined. The aim is to develop individual *autonomy* often symbolized by an apple with a bite taken out of it, the logo adopted by the city of New York as well as Apple Macintosh computers and software.

Eating disorders (bulimia, anorexia) are often the sign of a person seeking their *own identity*, who has a weak personality and is hypersensitive to an unsatisfactory affective environment (abandonment, or parental overprotection) which did not permit secure inner construction or independence (narcissistic disorders).

Gestalt Therapy—especially in a *group*, where the person concerned can *experiment* with these two needs of *confidence and autonomy*, at his own rhythm—is frequently more effective than any diet or speeches. The client is encouraged to affirm (assertively, calmly, and in public) his ideas, needs, preferences, and his own choices, both verbally and with specific enactment; he will define little by little his personal *boundaries*, without blindly "feeding off" the environment, and without global refusal. This sort of approach usually goes on with little or no reference to the eating disorders themselves.

Aggression

Aggression is of course indispensable to maintain *our place* in this world. It must not be confused with destructive *violence*. I like to recall its etymological significance: *ad-gressere (adgredere)* means "going in front of another" to meet him, just as *pro-gressere* means "going forward". These two words are the opposite of *re-gressere*: "go backwards". Positive aggression is the *conquest* of my environment (like eating): it is a way for me to be recognized, to exist (from *ex-sistere*, "place oneself outside"), and to affirm myself in space and time: I have a right to *my space and to my time*, by verbal, physical or social expression.

The difficulty comes when instead of fighting for *my* own legitimate space of existence, I try to invade another's! Such as when I move away from healthy *assertiveness*, which is strongly encouraged in Gestalt, towards domination or violence. We build our autonomous personality by *affirming* our own specific identity, by avoiding passive *submission* (without initiative), as well as by avoiding invasive *domination*, without respect for the neighbor's need to assert himself.

The pathway is narrow, and difficult. It usually implies four overlapping stages:

- Infantile *dependence*,
- *Counter-dependence*, or the self-affirming revolt in adolescence,
- Adult *independence*: I often agree—but *not always*—with my friends, my political party, my church.
- Mature *interdependence*: I am free . . . and others too! And so, I take my own needs *as well as* those of others, into consideration. Everybody needs others.

Healthy aggression is thus far from being a "death drive", or a "return to inanimate", according to Freud's[1] belated hypothesis. This hypothesis is by the way more and more strongly contested by the psychoanalytical community itself. *Ethological* studies, such as those performed by Lorenz, who observed animals in their natural environment, have largely confirmed that a healthy animal displays positive, controlled aggression. We know that in a litter of puppies, the calmer and most sweet natured are also the least healthy.

It is not the least of Perl's contributions, to have explicitly rehabilitated this theme in both psychology and therapy. Remember that his first work was called *Ego, Hunger and Aggression* (1942).

During a Gestalt Therapy session, the therapist does not hesitate, in certain situations, to deliberately stimulate a client's aggression: to help a shy, retiring person manifest his presence, to energize a depressed person, or "wake up" a masochist, etc. It is interesting to note that the aggression and sexuality regulatory zones are very close, and linked in the deep brain (hypothalamus), and that the *same* neurotransmitters (dopamine, testosterone, etc) control these two behaviors. Because of this, the therapist could use aggression as a type of "equivalent" to sexuality, when directly addressing the latter presents difficulties (ethical or deontological reasons). In fact we know that sexual difficulties are one of the most frequently evoked themes spontaneously brought up by clients in therapy. Thus for instance, a moment of physical combat is more acceptable in a group than an erotically explicit interaction! The deep emotional mobilization is, in reality, very close in both cases, and facilitates fresh, emotionally charged verbal sharing, which is just as involved.

Sexuality

Just as healthy utilization of honest and respectful aggression can be abused—which has led to a rejection of all aggression—the same applies to *sexuality* in our Western culture[2], due to similar abuse and misunderstanding: we "threw the baby out with the bath water"! Here yet again, common sense is sufficient to understand that it would be just as unreasonable to globally condemn it, as to condone it without reservation: neither fighting, ignoring, nor passively submitting to it, but "taming" it; neither gripping the steering wheel too tightly, nor letting go completely, but keeping two hands on it to "manage" how to drive it.

These days, it no longer seems necessary to stress that sexuality is not merely a *reproductive* function. This does not go against Nature's plan: she took the trouble to create specific *pleasure* organs, with dense local innervation and a range of neurotransmitters that mediate desire, excitation and well-being, which also shows that sexual activity plays a role in social and affective *relationships*.

A look at "multiple" sexualities

Diverse ideologies, customs and prejudices have always appro priated this particularly sensitive domain—which has often been used as a "weapon" by many powers: imperial, revolutionary, ecclesiastical, even medical. It is not the aim of this book to detail the sexual morals throughout the ages and regions, but a rapid visit in time and space certainly helps relativize certain aspects:

- *Sexual hospitality* was sacred in many historical nations: Egypt, Syria, Phoenicia, Cyprus and even today in the Eskimo culture. The Temple in Alexandria had 1,400 specific rooms for sacred prostitutes, available for worshippers and foreigners. Prostitutes were venerated, as are nuns today. In Phoenicia, the Law stipulated that all women belonged to all men and that no distinction should exist between fathers or between children.
- In the past, *anal intercourse* was as frequent as vaginal intercourse in heterosexual relations. The latter was punishable by death during maternal breastfeeding, in ancient pre-Colombian America. In Greece, "positions" were limited

to one prescribed posture: partners lying on their sides, one behind the other, like "spoons", as neither lover was supposed to "dominate" the other! Later, with the Catholics, the opposite principle justified the "missionary" position!

- A brief look at *polygamy*: In Gaul, clans of a dozen men or so (brothers, fathers and sons) shared the wives of the Britons who fought Caesar. The harem of the Chinese Emperors, until the end of the Empire, had 1,000 concubines—chosen by the Emperor's mother. The last Moroccan emperor, Moolay Ismaïl, sired 888 children. (The feminine record belongs to a Russian woman who had 69 babies, from 27 pregnancies.). Legend attributes 1800 mistresses to John Kennedy: he made love every day. Whereas, according to the latest detailed French government scientific report, on 20,000 people in France, from 18 to 70 years old (*Analysis of Sexual Behavior in France*, conducted by Professor Spira), in 1993, the "average" Frenchman had 13 sexual partners in his life, and the average French woman . . . 5! And less than 1% of men had relations with over 100 women. Of course it is an average, as sexual activity is very variable and increases with the level of education: those who undertake university study *double* the number of partners . . .
- In the *Middle Ages*, if a woman died in childbirth, the Catholic Church considered her to be a witch: she was impaled, with her "baby vampire", and forbidden burial in a cemetery! Right up until the 16th century, most parish priests had an official concubine (and the Pope preferentially ordained their sons priests).
- Each of the *Revolutions* (France, USSR, China, etc) began with sexual freedom—which liberated energy . . . and were followed by sexual coercion—which recuperates energy!
- Today in Iran, women are forbidden in swimming pools and in . . . buses! In communist Romania, women had to declare the dates of their menstruation to their employer—to avoid abortions . . . and in China, this is actually the case . . . to make them abort!
- *Freud* considered *clitoridian* pleasure as "immature" and many female psychoanalysts, including the Princess Bonaparte, had their clitoris implanted in the vagina . . . unsuccessfully! 4,000 women had this operation in the USA!

- In 1914, women went to see their doctor . . . if they *felt* sexual pleasure: female orgasm was considered to be a sign of "hysteria" or "perversion", and they faked . . . *not* reaching orgasm!
- Up until recently, *masturbation* was condemned. In fact, today it is considered by specialists as a *natural and necessary* stage of development, which prepares for sexual functioning, notably facilitating subsequent female orgasm. Lack of masturbation *doubles* the percentage of female *frigidity*, leading to conjugal dissatisfaction, even divorce: a "perverse effect" of the moral orders of abstinence!
- And so, today, at the age of 30, only 50% of French women reach *orgasm* in a "normal complete" sexual intercourse. Amongst the others, 75% attain orgasm with clitoral stimulation.

We could go on and on with this list of *arbitrary* moral variations and their consequences . . .

Remember the scandal provoked in 1948 by the publication of the famous *Kinsey Report* on human sexuality: his study, based on 15,000 Americans, showed that . . . 95% regularly practiced what were at the time qualified as "perverse" sexual practices! For instance: fellatio, cunnilingus, sodomy, etc. We know that in 1993, in France, 90% of men and 85% of women have tried oral sex at least once, and that this is practiced *regularly* today, half of the time.

Some rules, still taught from *ideological* principles, are completely *incoherent* with actual reality:

- Complete banning of *contraceptives*, if applied, would imply "death for all humanity": calculations show that within 200 years, the world population would reach the density of the metro at rush hour, over the whole surface of the earth! Only an atom bomb or an epidemic could save the planet! Fortunately, the impact of such rules is negligible (!)—as shown by scientific research which reveals little difference between practicing believers and agnostics. For example, today in France, 90% of women and 93% of men have their first sexual experience *before* marriage . . . and the same percentage also applies to young practicing Catholics.

And Gestalt Therapy, in all that?

What does Gestalt Therapy propose, concerning sexuality?

Specifically . . . nothing! Except, to avoid those poorly assimilated *introjections* from the external environment, whether they concern abstinence or "sexual liberation", and striving to be, at each moment, attentive to one's own needs as well as to those of others.

In fact, it is a matter of fostering an attitude of *tolerance,* accepting the *diversity of needs,* and questioning pre-established norms. Some are content with one sexual encounter each day, others with one each month, sometimes much less . . . or none at all! Some prefer homosexual relations, others avoid them, and may even be disgusted. All of this is "normal" . . . that's to say, there is no permanent, universal norm! Except *vigilance in respect for the other person*—who must be adult, responsible and consenting.

This acceptance of reality, free of ideological prejudice, this *tolerance of diversity,* has led many members of minority groups (homosexuals, for instance[3]) to feel at ease in Gestalt Therapy groups—where they feel they can openly express their personal, interpersonal and social patterns, needs and problems.

Liberalism is not laxness

This liberalism is sometimes wrongly interpreted as *laxness:* this is not the case! Any behavior is acceptable only if it makes *sense for the person concerned.* Be careful of fashions and counter-reactions: let's not condone a certain "anticonformistic neo-conformism", which consists of multiplying sexual experiences to "prove" one's freedom or to "be part of" a group! Freud thought that sexual *repression* was the origin of all *neuroses;* it would be pertinent to add that "sexual *overexpression*" can lead to a more serious *psychosis,* with a sense of loss of identity: I no longer know what I want, what I desire, or even who I am!

Sexual acting out

Sexual relations *between a client and his therapist* are *ethically forbidden,* whether during or outside sessions, during the whole of the therapy—and even after. It is *exactly this "safety" rule* that allows secure, in-depth exploration of sexual problems: desires, fantasies, lacks, satisfactions (the analysis of successes is just as therapeutic as that of failures). In addition, the unequal position of therapist and client risks damaging the therapeutic relationship.

However, in most Gestalt Therapy groups, this "rule of abstinence" does not apply to *participants between themselves*, who are considered *responsible* (as free adults, not mentally ill, etc.). Most group leaders and therapists frequently *point* out the dangers of the "group illusion" (Pages) which can lead to feeling that "we understand each other perfectly", "we are very close, with similar needs", etc., whereas this setting has been *artificially created* by the therapeutic context of acceptance and mutual confidence. We must not confuse *human love* with *sexual* love, *well-being* with *desire*, *letting go* with *no limits* . . . otherwise, beware of painful deception!

And then, a lax attitude would turn the personal growth of group participants away from its goal: some would come with the hope of finding a partner, rather than seeking the way forward on their own inner path.

However I would like to emphasize I do not agree with *formally forbidding* any sexual relations *between members* of a personal growth group. Experience shows that such an attitude is difficult to justify and maintain. In any case, the participants are supposedly *responsible* and it is exactly this very sense that Gestalt encourages! Also, prohibition implies surveillance—which is incompatible with the atmosphere of confidence, which is fundamental to every therapeutic group. It is preferable that the people concerned are able to *discuss* and even analyze their experience and its *significance* within the group, rather than having to hide it, which would imply abandoning the *authenticity*, which is necessary in every gestalt exchange.

Sexology

However you look at it, sexual difficulties, in every shape and form, are amongst the most frequently evoked themes, as much in individual therapy as in group work. Sexual difficulties are often a question of *affective* problems: relationship difficulties, boredom, feeling of being neglected, jealousy, etc., but also can be explicitly *sexological* problems: frigidity, sterility[4], impotence or premature ejaculation, disgust of certain practices expected by the partner, etc.

Paradoxically, most of these delicate problems are more easily discussed and treated in a *group* situation rather than in a *face-to-face individual* therapy, which is nevertheless more discrete.

Why is this? There are several reasons:

As soon as one member brings up such a problem, there are invariably similar echoes from others, and each one feels less alone, and less embarrassed. If one person cannot bring up such questions, it is likely that another will. The group greatly *dedramatizes* such situations. It also facilitates sharing of intimate feelings, rarely brought up[5], as well as providing a melting pot of original personal solutions.

The group is also a place to *experiment* with contact, with how one stimulates interest in others, as well as a minimum of confidence and tenderness, facilitating subsequent letting go with one's usual partner. It is also possible to "exorcise" rape and *sexual abuse* (some American statistics estimate that over 25% of women have had unsolicited sexual advances—mostly from a close friend or family member).

Here are some statistics that are not often talked about: one third of French women have frequent or occasional difficulty in reaching *orgasm*; while . . . 60% (!) of men suffer, more or less regularly, from *premature ejaculation*, and 20% admit erectile difficulties . . . but *each believes himself alone*, and never dares to talk about it! One of every 12 men is *impotent*[6] . . . yet only 10% of these men seek advice on the subject! This theme remains taboo in our Latin culture, and in France, there is virtually no native written literature, for the lay person, on the subject. Recently, the introduction of *Viagra, Cialis,* etc. helped a lot to speak about these problems.

During group therapy, simply *daring to speak* is often very efficient and liberating. Also, technical *information* can reassure and prepare the terrain for change. In fact, despite moral liberalization and freedom of the press (some specialized monthly magazines have phenomenal distribution!), ignorance remains the rule regarding many aspects of daily sexual life. One example: certain people still think of erection as a *muscular* phenomenon and that it can be *voluntarily* influenced, whereas it is an influx of blood, under the control of *two* distinct nervous systems, one of which integrates *physical* stimulation, and the other *psychological* fantasy (words, images, memories).

Fantasy and the couple

With Gestalt Therapy, we can rehabilitate the value of *fantasies* (which are specific to the human race) and also *free them from guilt*: we all have the right, in fact, to imagine the most unusual things: exhibitionism, sadomasochism, etc., nothing is forbidden, because by definition, fantasy is not reality! On the other hand, *sharing* fantasies with one's partner can be a strong sexual stimulant in many situations. The *absence* of fantasy, or their *confusion with reality*, are, by the way, classical signs of psychological problems.

During workshops reserved for *couples*, it is possible to enhance the relationship, to point out both common factors as well as *differences*, each one working in his partner's presence—who may discover, for example, that certain annoying habits are simply physiological: a man who falls asleep after lovemaking is not a boor, but simply . . . a man—whose blood, which was concentrated in the penis, returns to irrigate the rest of the body, thus provoking his relaxation, and neurotransmitter release . . .

We can also analyze the division of time and space in the couple: for instance, each draws—separately—where he feels truly at home in their house, or expresses unsaid desires . . . but we will not aim for the illusory "complete transparence", each has his right to a "secret garden". So-called "confessions" are more often weakness than honesty: in an effort to get rid of the heavy, cumbersome secret, it is revealed and placed at the partner's feet . . . and the conscience is clear! Unearthing all the roots of a tree, with "seeing how it grows" as an excuse, is usually a good way to get it to topple over!

If the couples' difficulties are deep and longstanding, it is not a question of temporarily "patching up" the problem at all costs, the appropriate approach may indeed be to explore how to negotiate *successful* separation, with as little damage as possible.

In practice

Couples workshops, sexuality workshops, or sessions dealing with any sort of problem, individual consultations, couples therapy, group therapy and personal development groups . . . Gestalt Therapy offers a *wide panorama of situations* that allow us to gain insight, and enrich how we experience different styles of contact and its uncertainties.

We can be confronted with various feelings and experiment, in a secure setting, new emotions: from shyness to aggression; from sexual inhibition to liberation, as well as all the usual difficulties. Gestalt therapy offers all the above, as well as continually patient and careful attention to the client's harmonious internal and social functioning—which is unique, respectful of his personal rhythm and individuality.

Notes

1. He was, at the time, suffering from jaw cancer.
2. This is not the case in many Oriental cultures: the *Tantra* for instance considers sexuality as the preferential path towards *spirituality*.
3. The percentage of homosexuals varies from 4% to 12% depending on age and location; it is greatest in large cities. *Male* homosexuals often have many partners: over 20 on average, but sometimes many hundreds, even *over a thousand!* The homosexual is in fact often "hypervirile", with testosterone over production, rather than "effeminate".
4. We have had many positive results in resistant cases of *female sterility*, with no apparent organic cause. Acceptance of the whole process from *nidation* through to *maternity* seem to be linked to tolerance and acceptance of the other, self-confidence and creativity.
5. Of course, one of the most fundamental rules in any therapeutic group, which facilitates meaningful exchange, is *absolute confidentiality* pertaining to everything that happens in the sessions (at least all that concerns those involved). Experience shows that "leaks" are exceptional.
6. *Impotence* is diagnosed when it is persistent and regular, over at least three months. Many *medicines* (Valium, Prozac, beta blockers, etc.) and *illnesses* (diabetes, etc.) can interfere with erection.

CHAPTER TEN

The Personality Profile
(Psychopathology)

Fundamental principles

Gestalt Therapy has developed with an existential and liberal perspective, according to which each human being is *unique and individual*. This philosophical viewpoint is thus *in principle* contrary to classification systems which tend to sort people into categories, and is opposed in particular to the traditional distinction between "normal" and "pathological."

That which is "normal" cannot be *statistically* defined, otherwise redheads ... or Gestalt Therapists would be "abnormal", simply because of their rarity! How can we define what is *socially* "normal", and yet avoid racism? Can homosexuals be considered "ill"? This idea, upheld in their day by Freud and Reich, is completely outdated now.

However, can we on the other hand consider a hallucinating schizophrenic to be "normal"?

Faced with such difficulties, orthodox Gestalt Therapists renounced all forms of *psychopathology*, especially as there is still no psychogenetic theory in Gestalt Therapy which would define "normal" phases of psychological growth. They hence preferred to seek the *individual meaning* of a "boundary phenomenon," which originates in the here and now, is unique to the moment, and to the given *field*.

A range of catalogues . . .

Taken to its extreme, this would mean that chronic "confluent people" or "projectors[1]" do not exist! However, as experience has shown us, some of us use a particular defense mechanism in a habitual, even stereotyped way. Should we then adhere to the theory of *antipsychiatry*[2] and from *ideological conviction*, ignore some very real problems?

Whatever the cause, personality disorders do *exist* whether we want them to or not! "The facts remain" and it is unreasonable to take the same approach with a suicidal depressive, an aggressive paranoiac or an excited histrionic.

In practice, each therapist, *consciously or not*, establishes his own diagnosis, according to the nosographic[3] criteria with which he is familiar. He then adapts his "therapeutic strategy" to each case.

Some Gestalt therapists try to elaborate a Gestalt interpretation of psychopathology, while most of them use *other classifications*, depending on their personal sensitivity, and cultural background, such as bio-energy (Reich and Lowen), psychoanalysis or the DSM IV (*Diagnostic and Statistical Manual* of mental disorders). This American nomenclature has been more or less adopted worldwide as it is purely *descriptive*, and is unrelated to any particular explicative theory.

Others suggest the creation of an *independent*, specifically Gestalt psychopathology, which would stem from the *Theory of Self* by Goodman.

I personally have developed a "transversal" approach since 1985— which takes into account many authors, including Freud, Klein, Jung, Horney, Bergeret, Kernberg, Guelfi . . . thus integrating many currents: *psychoanalytical*, neoreichian and *Gestalt Therapy*, without neglecting what traditional *psychiatry* and recent *neuroscientific* research has to offer.

In fact, it seems to me that setting up a *specific Gestalt psychopathology*—apart from the fact that many further studies would be required—would be, at the moment, markedly *premature* and would constitute a *strategic* error. The risk would be to widen the gap between Gestalt Therapists and their colleagues practicing psychiatry, psychology and psychoanalysis . . . at a time when Gestalt is still awaiting integration in universities and clinical psychiatry.

Already, each school of thought speaks a different jargon, which is not very clear for the others. Let's be careful of the paranoid all-powerful fantasy which incites each specialist to "reinvent the world" . . .

That's why I have deliberately chosen an attitude of *inter-disciplinary cooperation*, with reference to nosographic criteria that are already widely used *in France*, which I will attempt to summarize shortly.

I use traditional *nosographic descriptions* to start with, based on hundreds of studies and publications, yet without adhering to the *etiological hypotheses* of the various schools concerning the supposed *origin* of the problems . . . and even less so to their *therapeutic strategies*.

It is my opinion that Gestalt therapy proposes a *therapeutic attitude* that is often radically new. There is no doubt as to its therapeutic effect, yet Gestalt therapy does not aim to *explain the origin* of the disorders. It remains coherent with Perls' ideas, by refusing to stick to the sterile controversy between various schools of thought—especially as recent studies have introduced considerable uncertainty in psychopathology, which is really a new discipline, hardly out of the Stone Age.

Whatever the case, I certainly wish to avoid "labeling" the client, or classifying him within a pre-established collective compartment. I find this alienating, even arbitrary—remarks such as "Serge is obsessive" or "Jean is histrionic"; I prefer to build for each person an original personality "profile."

Let's take an example: international specialists are debating whether the loss of contact with reality in schizophrenia is caused by:

- Genetic predisposition (chromosomes 5 and 11),
- Biochemical disfunctionning of cerebral neurotransmitters (dopamine receptor disorder),
- Anatomical problems (in the prefrontal cortex),
- Precocious viral infection (recent hypothesis in which certain researchers believe),

- Maternal pathological attitude ("schizophrenogenic" overprotection, from traditional psychoanalysis, or Bateson's "double bind"),
- Or rather, a combination of many associated factors . . .

We really don't know! What's more, we don't really care!

Psychoanalysis with its sometimes *dogmatic* coherence contributed to hypotheses such as "paranoiacs are repressed homosexuals" . . . which merely satisfy the anxious mind's need to "understand"—or to arbitrarily combine often unrelated facts. Who can say for certain today whether the lack of excess of serotonin is the *cause* or the *consequence* of certain types of depression or obsessive neurosis?

After all, is it necessary to know all the details of the origin of a fracture (the circumstances of the accident, the victim's intentions, where and how it happened) to treat it? Such investigation may well be useful for future prevention, but does not help with first aid . . . It can even delay appropriate treatment.

I admit, with neither shame nor hesitation, that throughout extensive clinical practice, after 20 years of an intense psycho-analytical background, followed by more than 30 years of "passion" for Gestalt therapy, I have never had any major difficulty in adopting a strictly Gestaltist attitude to clients who have been labeled by psychiatrists with reference to traditional, non-Gestaltist nosography. After all, the psychopathological approach has two *separate* stages:

1. Nosographic research (diagnosis);
2. Therapeutic intervention (personalized treatment);

For the moment, Gestalt therapy is usefully applied to the second step . . . That's already a lot!

The basic personality

According to Freud, the two fundamental drives in Man are *sexuality* and *aggression* (*Eros* and *Thanatos*, or *life drive* and *death drive*). Anxiety stems from the dissatisfaction of archaic sexual needs. All the neuroses come from *sexual* function disturbance, whether real or symbolic. Reich links them more directly to orgasmic dissatisfaction.

According to Karen Horney (one of Perls' analysts, who had a great influence on him), as well as many existentialists, man—from birth—suffers from a *basic "existential anxiety."* We can thus consider sexuality and aggression as two *life* drives, or survival instincts (survival of the species, as well as of the individual). Neuroses and psychoses could thus be considered as *defenses against this fundamental anxiety.*

Whereas, for Freud and Melanie Klein, anxiety is considered one of the *consequences* of sexuality and aggression, Karen Horney takes the *opposite* standpoint and views sexuality as a *healthy* reaction against anxiety.

Basic Anxiety

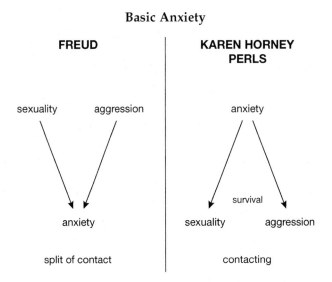

Defense mechanisms

Schematic or metaphoric examples of defense mechanisms and reassurance against *basic anxiety*:

- In autism: I withdraw from the outer world and I live an inner life;
- In paranoia: I am wary of everyone and everything; I attack before being attacked;
- In obsessive neurosis: I organize everything, to avoid being taken unaware;
- In hysteria: I seduce my environment and adapt myself to it, to create allies.

Personality "disorders" could thus be considered as mechanisms of *defense and adaptation*, which facilitate survival *at a given time*. However, when they become habitual and continue in an excessive, rigid way, they are not only *anachronistic* but also *cumbersome*: my coat of armor is no longer necessary when I leave the battlefield. In fact, it limits my movements and weighs on me: instead of helping, it hinders. The cure becomes worse than the illness.

Therapy

Therapy consists of *identifying* those defenses or resistances which are useful and *adapted* to the current environment, as well as those which are *out-of-date* or *rigid*.

The informed therapist is careful to evaluate the usefulness of his client's defenses: for instance, obsessive behavior, methodological and well-organized, often rigid and repetitive, sometimes including cleaning rituals, can usefully compensate for a deeper underlying anxiety. A direct attack on the symptoms and rituals risks revealing this fundamental anxiety, which will mobilize deeper, weightier defenses—such as paranoia. To be quite clear, the *apparent* problem must not be removed without adequate precautions.

Practically speaking, what can be done in the Gestalt Therapy approach?

We could, for instance, exploit the Gestalt notion of *polarities* and try to balance the tendencies: encourage the histrionic to obsessive behavior (times, dates, planning, organization, notes, etc.); the obsessive to "hysterize" (flexibility, improvisation, seduction, contact, emotional expression, artistic activities, etc.); the masochist to express his healthy aggression, to affirm his *assertiveness*, etc.

We can clearly see the richness of the Gestalt approach here. *Experimenting* new attitudes is possible in *regular on-going group workshops.* This *safe, secure environment* offers what Winnicott called a "transitional space" between external reality and the inner world of the client or the group, just as with sports, games or artistic pursuits. *Real* fighting and physical contact such as hugging may occur, but within a framework of specific, well-defined rules.

The client is accompanied in the progressive exploration of his diverse facets, guided by the three "pillars" of Gestalt therapy: *awareness, "presentification" (being in the here and now), responsabilization* (Naranjo).

One final remark: it is far from proven that all the *personality traits* evolve towards a neurotic disorder of the *same* type. Often, on the contrary, discrete tendencies function as "safety valves," and *prevent* the development of pathological troubles. For instance, ordinary phobias, like fear of mice or spiders, can sometimes be enough to canalize and manage an underlying anxiety. *Symptomatic* behavioral treatment, aiming only to eliminate the symptoms, can even be *contraindicated.* Similarly, mild "histrionic" manifestations, such as enjoying being admired, or needing to seduce, can help maintain *vital narcissism,* and prevent permanent *pathological* histrionic excitation from setting in; obsessive traits can *protect* against depression or paranoia . . .

In many cases, when the client "decompensates"—i.e. his usual defense mechanisms "break down" (which can lead to delirium, mutism, depression, sometimes suicidal) following fatigue, psychological trauma, charlatan "therapeutic" treatment, etc.—it comes as a surprise to the uninformed that sometimes the apparent troubles *disappear* and *new* or opposite troubles appear, often *more serious.*

I will never forget how my assistant at the Institute I directed abandoned his system of obsessive and hyper-organized defense (which made him an excellent supervisor), during a clumsy traditional psychoanalysis . . . and he ended up hospitalized for life with paranoid delirium with severe acting out: the analyst had indeed "cured" him of his obsessive habits of control and organization!

It is clear that careful training in psychopathology as well as regular clinical *supervision*[4] are essential to therapeutic practice.

The vigilant Gestalt therapist will always evaluate the creative and adaptive function of the behavior in question *(creative adjustment),* which may not only be quite *acceptable*, but also characteristic of the client's *original personality*. Or on the contrary, evaluation may reveal just how *problematic* the symptoms are for the client—or for his family!

The Personality Wheel (Ginger, 1989)

Brief explanation

- We attempted to *simplify* to a maximum; the wheel is based on two crosses: the Greek cross + (so-called "psychotic" axes) and the St Andrew's cross: x (so-called "neurotic" axes).
- The "psychotic" axes correspond to a *breach of contact with environmental reality*, in mental processes (paranoia and schizoidia), and in affective processes (bipolar disorder).

- The "neurotic" axes correspond to a *distorted relationship* to the environment.
- *Phobias* are not included in the diagram: they lie along the neurotic hysteria-obsession axis.
- The *Borderline* personality is characterized by the excessive presence of many different traits, with *unpredictable* movement from one to another: they may be histrionic, depressive then paranoid, one after the other . . . with impulse-driven *acting out* (separation, accident, suicide, etc.).

Suggestions for use
(if you would like to trace your own profile)

- Subjectively evaluate the importance of each of your *personality traits,* along each axis, from the center (absence of trait) to the circumference (pathologically pronounced trait).
- Join the points thus marked out, to obtain your own *specific psychological profile.*
- *Normality* (the healthy person) is *not the absence* of all traits (this would be a "poor" personality), but a relatively *balanced presence of each of them.*
- Thus, a "normal" person could simultaneously display *light* traits of:
  — "paranoia": he is self-affirming, defends his ideas (without being rigid), defends his principles, is prudent and vigilant (yet neither mistrustful nor naïve), is sensitive (but not hypersensitive), defends the downtrodden, etc. *(e.g. militant in a union, ..)*
  — "obsession": he is organized and careful; attentive to time and space, reliable, hard-working, etc.
  (e.g. the craftsman or the technician, . . .)
  — "hysteria": he is open to environmental ambiance and to others, sympathetic, good at listening, emotional, he likes to please, etc.
  (e.g. salesperson, actor, . . .)
  — "masochism": he has the capacity of devotion, he is capable of delayed gratification, etc.
  (e.g. social worker, or the "saint," . . .)

— "sadistic" domination: he has a self-affirming personality, initiative, a sense of responsibilities, etc *(e.g. the boss, . . .)*
— "depression": he will not seek refuge in "naïve optimism," he is "realistic," etc
(e.g. the existential *philosopher, . . .*)
— "mania" (in the psychiatric sense): he is hyperactive, always alert, etc.
(e.g. the entrepreneur, the deputy, . . .)
— "schizoid": he can assume loneliness, be introverted, etc.
(e.g. the researcher or the "wise man," . . .)

• This profile can be established with *collaboration between therapist and client*. From time to time, it is possible to *reevaluate*, without reference to previous profiles, to compare them and discuss during sessions, in order to better adjust therapeutic objectives.

To amuse yourself, you could compare your profile to the two "Masters," often evoked in this book, that I permitted myself to caricaturize!

Freud's "profile"

Perls' "profile"

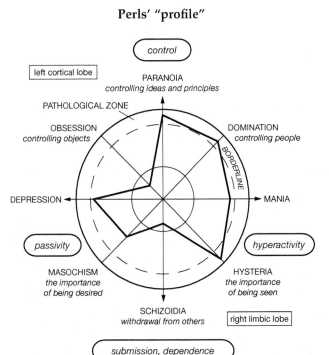

Notes

1. See Chapter 4, *Theory of Self and Resistances.*
2. According to which society is responsible for the madness it engenders and must therefore accompany the patient in his "plunge," rather than locking him away and treating him?
3. *Nosography:* methodological description and classification of problems and illnesses.
4. Regular, confidential checking of current treatment by a qualified specialist. When starting work with a therapist, it is a good idea to ensure that they are *certified* in their discipline, that they belong to a professional *association* (continuing Education) and that they undergo regular *supervision*. If they refuse to reply, information may be obtained from a professsional society or regulatory body.

CHAPTER ELEVEN

Twenty Basic Notions[1]

F or the impatient readers (those who begin by the end), I recapitulate here some main notions already developed in this book.

On March 14, 1970, Fritz Perls, "founding father" of Gestalt Therapy, died in Chicago. What remains of his heritage more than 35 years later, as we are now in the third millenium?

More precisely, what is specifically "Gestalt" in the current practice of the French Gestalt therapists of different tendencies ?

Which basic principles are still applied ? Which seem neglected, indeed even outmoded or obsolete, in the face of progress in theoretical and clinical research (Systems theory, Neurosciences, Sexology, etc), of the contributions from more recent related methods (Palo Alto School, Neuro-Linguistic Programming, etc.), or, more simply of the evolution in mores ("sexual revolution" and contraception, "1968 revolution", telematics, etc.) ?

These are some of the questions we want to explore. In so doing, we deliberately adopt a subjective and committed point of view. This conforms to what we think is essential in Gestalt Therapy philosophy itself, which is deeply marked by the existentialist values of freedom to be and to express oneself while respecting the originality of each individual.

We will use traditional documents: works by Perls and Goodman; interviews with From; the writings of Levitsky, Simkin, Zinker, Polster, Latner, Yontef, Miller; as well as many articles from the *Gestalt Journal*. But above all we will rely on our personal experience from 35 years of Gestalt clinical practice and 25 years of teaching at the *Paris School of Gestalt* (*École Parisienne de Gestalt*: EPG).

Here we will leave aside the techniques, the "rules and games" (often used, more or less advisably, out of their original context), and try to draw out a few basic notions; above all, we will deal with the contemporary evolution of these notions and seek out how they are related to each other. These relationships underline the *coherence* of the Gestalt method within the context of a philosophy of Man.

I will mention these basic notions in a somewhat arbitrary order for they all seem to me to be linked and interdependent, operating in a "circular" mode, (numbered cross-references will make it easier to see these correlations).

1. Now and How 2. Process 3. Awareness 4. Contact-boundary 5. Field and System 6. Creative Adjustment 7. Experience Cycle 8. Unfinished Business 9. Resistances 10. Homeostasis 11. Toward a sense of Responsibility 12. Experimentation 13. Right to Difference, the Individual's Originality 14. Sympathy Attitude 15. A Holistic approach to Man 16. Complementary Polarities 17. Emotional and Bodily Implications 18. Aggression 19. Creativity and Imagination 20. The Individual in the Group

1. "Now and how"

Perls' expression "now and how" seems better than the classic expression "here and now", which is far from being specific to Gestalt. In fact, many other methods focus on the "here and now" process: the Rogerian approach, the main group psychotherapies and even psychoanalysis—since it works above all on transference, which is supposed to reproduce infantile neurosis "here and now".

On the other hand, "now and how" underlines the specifically *phenomenological* aspect of Gestalt Therapy which gives greater place to the *how* than to the *why*, and puts the accent on describing phenomena rather than on explaining them: "One should come back from a discourse on things to the things themselves, such as they truly appear at the level of real facts, prior to any distorting conceptual elaboration" (Husserl, 1907). Phenomenology underlines the importance of *subjective* and irrational factors, of immediate real-life experience and its bodily experience (see n° 17), which is unique to each individual (n° 13). The *how* is revealed in particular in unconscious posture, gestures or "micro-gestures," in the way of breathing, in voice intonation, etc. The implicit *modalities* of behavior and of talk often prevail over their explicit *content*: thus, Perls, as Lacan later on, underlines a pre-eminence of the *signifier* over the *signified*.

Of course, the work on the *now* in no way precludes evoking memories, fears or projects—providing that they emerge spontaneously, consciously or not, from the client: they are present *now* in his mind or in his heart and nourish his present-day life. Moreover they are inevitably modulated by the existing context (internal or external to the client) and therefore are never plain "historical truths."

The too zealous Gestaltists who at all costs try to maintain their client in the narrow "prison of the present" are naive. On the other hand, contrary to traditional psychoanalytical strategy, the client will not be prompted to seek out past memories, to undertake long "archaeological excavations," as Perls says. It is best to settle in first on the "ground-floor" of one's house and arrange one's existing "living-room," before attempting to clear out all the rubbish accumulated in the cellar . . . which may take several long years, as everyone knows! One will always be able to put the finishing touches on the cleaning—if the traces of the past continue to be bothersome. But when that moment arrives, one will at least have accumulated the energy of the present.

2. Process

Thus, the *process* remains foremost: the therapist and his client remain above all vigilant and attentive (cf. n° 3: Awareness) to the fluctuations of the relationship which is developing "here and now": Perls *(The Gestalt Approach)* liked to ask four basic questions, centered on the ongoing process:

- What are you doing now ?
- What are you feeling now ?
- What are you trying to avoid ?
- What do you want, what do you expect from me?

This constant attention to the current development of the situation remains rather specific to Gestalt Therapy which is readily interested in immediately perceptible *surface phenomena*. Obviously, one most often leaps from the present toward the past and descends from the surface toward the depths. In the same way, the study of the membrane gives to the contemporary biochemist a great deal of information on the cell's overall functioning, and the analysis of the actual radiance sent out by a distant star gives an astrophysicist information on past events which occurred long ago.

Thus, the Gestalt Therapist and his client are constantly involved in a coming and going, a "shuttle" (as Perls says) between present and past, between internal fantasies (*intrapsychic*) and external behavior and *interpsychic* relationships, between nonverbal expression and speech, between emotion and realization, as "figures" successively emerge on the "ground" of the *continuum* of consciousness—as Gestalts come into being and are destroyed. We will return to this theme again, in connection with the unfolding of self during the *experience cycle* (cf. n° 7 and 8).

3. Awareness

This multivalent attention, this deliberate and preconscious vigilance—intellectual, emotional, bodily—concentrated on one's intimate and subjective *internal* experience and on the *external* environment (also subjectively perceived); this "immediate awareness" of the present in all its dimensions, is sought in Zen Buddhism ("Buddha" means "one who is awakened") as well as in Gestalt—where it is defined by the word *awareness*. When Perls was asked to sum up Gestalt in a single word, that is the one he would generally mention, whereas nowadays many Gestalt therapists prefer the term *contact*.

4. Contact boundary

Goodman's basic work on Gestalt Therapy, written in 1951 and based on Perls' notes, starts with these two words. Perls, in *The Gestalt Approach* (posthumously published in 1975) takes up this idea again: "The study of the way the human being functions in his environment is the study of what goes on at the boundary between the individual and his environment. It is at this contact boundary that the psychological events take place". And Goodman points out: "The contact-boundary, where experience occurs, does not *separate* the organism and its environment; rather, it limits the organism, contains and protects it, and *at the same time* it touches the environment [. . .] for example, the sensitive skin is not so much a part of the "organism" as it is essentially *the organ of a particular relation of the organism and the environment"*. Boundary therefore "belongs" at the same time to the internal and the external spheres of experience: it belongs to two distinct but interrelated worlds.

"Psychology is the study of creative adjustment", Goodman says again, "correspondingly, abnormal psychology is the study of the interruption, inhibition, or other accidents in the course of creative adjustment". The disruptions of the contact or "resistances" (cf. n° 9) may all be considered as boundary problem: abolition of the clear demarcation in case of excessive *confluence* with the environment, "overflowing" of the external or internal world in case of *introjection* or *projection,* etc., as shown in the graph of the chap. 4, p. 37 (see also n° 9).

5. Field and system

During a therapy session, one of the main elements of the client's "environment" is the *therapist* himself. It is with him that the contact is established and that the interaction process, with all its fluctuations, is engaged. Client and therapist, then, are part of the same "field" of experience and each one's attitude interferes with that of the other. It is not of course a "closed system," but an "open" one, in a permanent exchange with the external *context.*

In *Gestalt Therapy,* Goodman takes up the reflections of Kurt Lewin who had just extrapolated Maxwell's theory of the electromagnetic field, generalized by Einsteinian physics, into the social field. These works were also nourished by Minkowski's phenomenological conceptions about psychological space-time. Nowadays, this *Field Theory* is often integrated into the *System Theory* which proposes an interdisciplinary and methodological conceptualization. It is to be distinguished from *holism,* which holds, somewhat naively, that the knowledge of the whole explains the function of each part. Edgar Morin (*La Méthode de la Méthode,* 1977) has indeed underlined how holism, thought to have gone beyond reductionism, has, in fact, brought about a "reduction to the whole," eliminating complexity in favor of an "euphoric" notion of wholeness. But "whole is a hole".

Gestalt therapy is interested in each one within his environmental context, being careful, at the same time, neither to isolate him artificially, nor to "merge" him in the global field. It closely follows the succession of the original emergence of each "figure" on the ground.

6. Creative adjustment

Mental and social "health" finds its expression in a permanent "creative adjustment" at the "contact-boundary" between organism and environment; particularly between the individual, the therapist and the actual context (area where interaction takes place, presence of witnesses or of a group, etc.). It is not a question of a simple adaptative "adjustment" in which the individual *is subjected* to the environmental law, adopting majority social norms or behavior generally considered "normal". Nor is it a question of individual creativity which would take absolutely no account of the context and would allow any whims or excesses—on the simple pretext that they suit the client. Indeed, it is a compromise, or rather a synthesis allowing each one to exist as he sees fit, but taking into account local and temporal norms so as to find his own way within a whole. In this way, Gestalt Therapy is distinguished from behavioristic theories which tend to be more normative: in a deliberately *phenomenological* perspective, it gives a greater place to each one's subjective experience, to what each person feels internally, than to socially perceptible external behavior. For all that, Gestalt Therapy does not confine itself to the sole "intrapsychic" fantasy life, but encourages the shuttle between the internal and the external trying to reconcile social adaptation and individual creativity, the situation and the "personal reading" of it, thus proposing a bridge between science and art.

Here, the socio-political context within which Gestalt Therapy developed should be recalled: Perls, Goodman and a few other pioneers of the 50s, definitely wanted to distinguish themselves from the American psychoanalytic establishment, portraying themselves as nonconformists in a particularly provocative way: pronounced anarchistic opinions, as well as "anarchistic" social and sexual behavior. Nowadays, Gestalt Therapy has "adjusted" itself to the "post 68"[2] context and has become greatly "subdued", though still keeping a liberal connotation.

7. Experience cycle

Each individual's action or relational interaction unfolds in several stages. These make up the "experience cycle"—also called, depending on the authors: "contact-withdrawal cycle" or "needs' satisfaction cycle." Perls and Goodman distinguished four main stages: *forecontact, contacting, final contact* and *post-contact* (or *withdrawal*). Since Perls' death, some authors have refined the usual interrelation sequences and now distinguish five, six, or even seven stages in the cycle: emergence or sensation, realization or awareness, excitation or energy mobilization, contact and enactment, interaction or fulfillment, withdrawal or experience assimilation (Zinker, 1977; Katzeff, 1978), or: forecontact, engagement, full contact, disengagement, assimilation (Ginger, 1989).What interests us here is the very principle of the succession of phases.

This classic cycle, though, does not always unfold in a regular way: we have already underlined (cf. n° 4) that, for Perls and Goodman "abnormal psychology is the study of the interruption, inhibition, or other accidents in the course of creative adjustment". Such disruptions of the functioning of the self are generally called "resistances" (cf. 9). They may build up defense mechanisms appropriate to the situation ("resistance-adaptation" of the Polsters) or anachronistic and rigid blocks which testify to a pathological functioning of genuine contact avoidance.

During the cycle, the self functions according to various successive "modes" (id, ego, "middle mode", personality) which dominate alternatively. Because of the brevity of this article we will not describe these different functioning modes—which may be disrupted or even be missing.

8. Unfinished businesses

Normally, once a (psychic or behavioral) action is completed, we are ready for a new one: this is the uninterrupted succession of *Gestalten*, in formation and destruction, that makes up the *continuum of consciousness* of each person "in good psychic health" and that functions in a continuous flow.

When the cycle has not fully played itself out, the situation may remain *unfinished* and become a pre-conscious element of internal pressure—a mobilizing element or one which may cause a neurosis. Thus, for example, an unfinished task (a lesson to be learned, the savoring of a slice of bread interrupted by a phone call, an outing frustrated by a thunderstorm, . . .) may remain "present" waiting only for the first opportunity to play themselves out. This is called the *Zeigarnik effect* (from Gestalt psychologist Bluma Zeigarnik who studied it under Lewin). In some other situations though, this pressure may be transformed into a haunting and exhausting psychic tension which becomes in the long run a source of neurosis (ill-accepted bereavement or separation, sustained unemployment, chronic sexual dissatisfaction, repeated failure in exams, etc).

The work on unfinished businesses is a typical example of attention being paid, in Gestalt Therapy, to vestiges from the past which interfere with the present: it is not a question of magically getting rid of an internal burden through the enactment of a type of psychodrama, but much rather of integrating this burdensome element of one's life into a significant whole, as one of the "polarities" in the life of the client (cf. 16).

9. Resistances

We have already mentioned on several occasions the interruptions or blocks in the "normal" development of the cycle which generally create disruption of the contact function (with part of oneself or with another person). It should be pointed out that *inhibition of action* (Laborit, 1979) does not necessarily imply dysfunction: on the contrary, it may be a defense mechanism or an urgent response well adapted to the situation. Thus, *confluence* with a loved one is part of being in love and *retroflection* of an anger against my boss may protect me from a possible dismissal. Only anachronistic, rigid and repetitive mechanisms express pathological functioning. First they must be spotted, and next made more flexible or transformed during psychotherapy.

The word "resistance" is used with another meaning in psychoanalysis (unconscious resistance to treatment linked to psychic functioning). Furthermore, it often retains a negative connotation—which led several authors to seek other terms. By analogy, it should be noted that it is the electric "resistance" that turns power into light or heat; it is the resistance of materials that allows a bridge to fulfill its function and again, it is the Resistance[3] that allowed us to safeguard our national identity during World War II.

Perls distinguished four main "resistances" which we will not describe in detail in this paper: *confluence, introjection, projection* and *retroflection*. But during the last twenty years various authors have suggested broadening this range with various combinations such as *deflection* (Polster), *proflection* (Sylvia Crocker), egotism, invalidation . . .

10. Homeostasis

We can recognize in Perls the optimistic and Rousseauistic belief in the satisfying self-regulation of the organism. The general principle of *homeostasis* had been set out by Cannon as early as 1926. Henri Laborit, for his part, distinguishes *generalized* homeostasis (that of the whole organism with regard to the milieu) and *restricted* homeostasis (preserving the equilibrium of the internal milieu itself).

With the advent of organ transplants and the appearance of AIDS, the sufficiency of natural defenses was somewhat questioned, and homeostasis is no longer so dominant a theme for most contemporary Gestalt therapists. There remains nevertheless the implicit postulate, widely developed by the movement known as "Humanistic Psychology," according to which each individual has all the potential he may need within himself. This idea can be recognized in most forms of medicine known as "parallel" or "alternative" medicines: acupuncture, homoeopathy, naturotherapy, etc.

Some Gestalt therapists maintain a blind faith in the interplay of energetic equilibriums, with a deliberately and optimistic "transpersonal" connotation. Homeostasis would not only be "intrapersonal" to each one, nor "interpersonal" between the members of a given group, but global, following "transpersonal" cosmic laws and transcending human and social consciousness.

11. Toward a sense of responsibility

Perls attached great importance to each one's responsibility ("response-ability") and his therapy aimed at self-support, behavioral and decision-making autonomy. Gestalt takes great care to avoid, as much as possible, any alienation of the client. Accordingly, the therapist does not remain distant and "walled" in the enigmatic attitude of the one who is "supposed to know." He shares with his client his feeling and his questioning (that is the therapeutic exploitation of counter-transference, cf. 14). The client, rather than being a passive "patient" who undergoes a treatment which is partly "esoteric" for him, is a full partner, even indeed a "co-therapist," who takes part in his own treatment.

The therapist, then, avoids setting up or maintaining the client in a "transference neurosis" which would make him relive his infantile dependence. Transference phenomena are generally identified and exploited as they come up, so as to avoid any kind of lasting alienation and facilitate an acceptance of responsibility. Perls and his contemporaries readily condemned the expression "I cannot", proposing to replace it by "I don't want," thus emphasizing the responsibility of each person in his own behavior.

Nowadays this semantic rule is not so widely applied, in particular by those in Gestalt who have to deal with borderline cases, even with psychotics. This rule seems to deny the importance of unconscious mechanisms. Moreover, it should indeed be acknowledged that "limping is not sinning" (Lucien Israël) and that not everybody is capable of assuming all his difficulties right away. This implies, if need be, periods of therapeutic support, an artfully balanced alternation of frustrations and gratifications, until the client may really do without a "prop." When a car's battery is flat, it may be necessary to hook it up to a mechanic's battery temporarily until it has regained the minimum energy necessary for self-functioning.

12. Experimentation

Rather than searching patiently for hypothetical *causes* of disorders, Perls substitutes an experimental search for *solutions*: it is not a question of "knowing why" but of "experiencing how" through eventual metaphorical enactments. Enactment favors realization, awareness, through a tangible action "re-presented" and experienced in all its "polarities" (n° 6). It thus contrasts with the impulsive or defensive "acting out", which psychoanalysis has rightly denounced, because, on the contrary, it short-circuits awareness by substituting action with verbal analysis.

The French language has only one word to express the "active" form of experimentation (*to experiment*) and its passive form (*to experience*); but an experiment can be *carried out* and a lived feeling can be experienced, such as rejection or loneliness for instance. Experimentation allows to "taste before swallowing" to struggle against parental and social commands (you have to"; "you must") and to avoid nourishing the introjections that paralyze our spontaneity and hamper our originality . . . including, of course, the introjection of new norms that Gestalt therapists insidiously propose such as " 'you must' should be banned" (*double-bind*), "free your emotions," "seek fulfillment for your needs" (egotism), etc. In fact, each person experiences for himself what suits him, according to his history, education, social milieu and ideological options. Time and again, Perls himself denounced those who identified with him, sometimes even copying his faults and mannerisms. This seems to be an inevitable temptation for students naive enough to think that by copying their master's habits they will appropriate his genius, such as those among Lacan's disciples who sport a bow tie and manipulate French grammar with too much ease.

Today, during training, each future therapist is encouraged to seek out his own style by experimenting with various attitudes consistent with his own way of being. It is not a question of seeking out an abstract orthodoxy through "well-tested" techniques (rigid *Gestalten*) but rather of creating one's own approach with a good deal of experimentation by trial and error—while, of course, respecting the method's basic principles.

13. Right to difference, the individual's originality

In this way, Gestalt Therapy emphasizes the right to difference and stresses the value of each one's specificity in a resolutely existentialist and nonconformist perspective. Today's Gestalt therapists, for the most part, can hardly be considered as anarchistic militants—as were Perls and Goodman—but they have faithfully upheld the cult of free expression for each individual, of vigilant respect for their clients' rhythms and diversified needs, of the specific growth of every human being—who preserves an area of freedom despite the fact that he is conditioned both historically and geographically by his past and his environment. Indeed,

what matters is not what has been done with me,
but what I do with what has been done with me[4]

What constitutes my human dignity is my own original approach to my own life.

Therefore the therapist does not systematically seek in each client a stereotyped succession of developmental stages or of existential crises—supposed to make up the common ground of all humanity. I am the one who gives a meaning to each action of my life, combining "given" and "imparted" meaning. If I wish to change, it is by remaining myself, differently myself, but not other than myself: this is the famous "paradoxical theory of change" enunciated by the Gestalt therapist Arnold Beisser (1970), who in fact has developed an idea previously expressed in 1956 by Carl Rogers. This "navigating with the stream" (*Don't push the River*, as Barry Steven puts it) is recommended by Gestalt Therapy, which even encourages, if need be, the amplification of the symptom and not its sedation. Thus, for example, psychosomatic outward signs of anguish may be encouraged so as to "allow the bodily unconscious to speak", and consequently make itself better heard—even indeed, better seen— through a magnifying effect. Here it is a question of combining the cathartic effect of emotional expression with the emergence of personal associative clues, absolutely refusing to paste on interpretations suggested from the outside by the therapist. This respect for the originality of each person's psychic functioning is one of the touchstones of the Gestalt approach. It can also be found in the work done on dreams, where any systematic reference to archetypal symbolism is excluded.

14. "Sympathy" attitude

The Gestalt Therapist therefore accompanies his client attentively and shares with him the uncertainties and joys of the successive discoveries made in the course of a venturesome expedition within a particular and ill-known territory. He is not a "specialist" who knows beforehand all the maps of the psychic regions.

He neither takes refuge in an attitude of neutral withdrawal, albeit kindly, nor is he obliged to accompany his client everywhere, in an "unconditional acceptance" of his excessive risks, or, on the contrary, of his repetitive avoidance. He is an experienced fellow traveller, who actively takes part in the client's internal progress. If need be, he shares his sensations, his feelings, his astonishments, his impatient attitudes, his satisfactions, and keeps a close watch to see the effect this sharing may have on his fellow traveller.

It is this attitude of "sympathy" that Perls opposes, in a somewhat caricatured way, to psychoanalytic "apathy" and to Rogerian "empathy." I am here, facing you (or more often beside you): I am neither elsewhere, in a cognitive world, nor in your place, stirred by your own emotions, but myself, in relation with you, in a genuine sharing between two people, in a "I/thou" dialogical relation (Buber, 1923). It is the constant analysis of what is now developing in the *"in between,"* on the contact-boundary between client and therapist, that makes up the very heart of the therapy.

The frequent sharing of the Gestalt practitioner's personal feeling, and the deliberate exploitation of his counter transferential experience are major tools, quite specific to Gestalt psychotherapy (cf. Juston, 1990). Perls would readily use them in a somewhat "wild" way, as a very direct mobilizing provocation. Most contemporary therapists, aware of the obvious risks brought about by any excess of spontaneity—aggressive as well as affective—have largely watered down Perls' acid wine and pay careful attention to the way they express their counter transference (which is thoroughly analyzed—with no *a priori* mistrust—during supervision or control meetings). Accordingly, I neither say nor show *all* that I feel, but I nevertheless exploit it to the maximum and share what I think might be useful to the therapy's development.

15. A holistic approach to man

All available languages are used in this continuous client-therapist-client dialogue: speech, but also posture, every gesture and semi-conscious "micro-gestures", explicit or underlying emotions. Rather than to a wild and uncontrolled "do it all," the psychoanalytic "basic rule" of the "say it all" has been expanded to an "express it all" through various means: bodily motion, even a possible bodily contact (rather unusual in individual therapy but common practice in group therapies), use of the environment (the metaphorical exploitation of various objects).

Associations proceed freely, according to the mode preferred by each person, at any given moment: from body to emotion, from emotion to verbal language, from verbal language to social inter-action—or on the contrary: from social phenomena to their verbal-ization, from word to emotion, from lived emotion to its bodily expression.

Man is viewed as a whole, in the systemic interaction of his five main "dimensions"—physical, affective, rational, social and spiritual —encompassing the whole being in all of its local and cosmic environment, in search of a fundamental meaning (cf. *Ginger's Pentagram*, 1983).

16. Complementary polarities

The holistic view of man in his field implies a multidirectional view—inward and outward—according to each of the axes that have been drawn out and toward each of its extremities.

The necessary search for equilibrium cannot be satisfied with a never-ending homeostatic re-adjustment—necessarily conservative—which can only lead toward an "unjust middle-way", mythical space, dull and narrow, where initiative and innovation are castrated. The equilibrium of each living being is a changing combination of life and survival mechanisms, which ensure "change within continuity." Just as a tight-rope walker keeps his balance by moving, helped by the length of his balancing pole, a Gestalt therapist will advocate the new experience of a moving ahead accompanied by the exploration of the opposed but complementary extremes: introjection/projection, adaptation/creation, submission/revolution, introversion/extraversion, love/hate, tenderness/aggression, frustration/gratification. . . . The list of opposite and complementary attitudes and experiences that a client may live by experiment and "experience" in the course of his individual or group therapy would be endless.

The objective is not to go deeper into each choice with the illusory purpose of choosing "the best" and of restricting oneself to an ideal "menu", but rather to savor the inexhaustible richness of *à la carte* meals, which would be suited to one's appetite and to those with whom one might be eating at a given time.

Perls had a liking for the work on polarities, particularly through the "monodrama"[5] technique with the inversion of roles.

17. Emotional and bodily implications

The interplay of complementary polarities may be symbolized by the cooperation of our brain's two hemispheres. Today we know that, contrary to a still widespread idea, the left side of the brain, analytic, rational and verbal, is not the "dominant" one (though it is the one that controls speech) and it is under the control of the synthetic, emotional, imaginary and nonverbal right side of the brain. Perls had a hint of this when he exhorted us to a revolution: "Lose your head, come to your senses!." We know also that this right brain is not feminine but masculine (geared by testosterone).

Contemporary Gestalt Therapists no longer follow him completely in his strong reactions: escaping the "hemiplegia" our culture advocates (which censures and atrophies our right hemisphere) does not imply "losing one's head", but, on the contrary, bringing it into unison with the heart and body. Thirty five years after its founder's death, Gestalt Therapy still suffers from Perls' affected contempt for any kind of theorization—which he was quite ready to label as "bullshit", and many are those who still deplore this method's conceptual backwardness. This judgment is obviously exaggerated and a good many detractors criticized mainly what they do not know. It is true though that the several hundred publications on Gestalt cut a sorry figure compared to the thousand works which enhance psychoanalysis . . . while at the same time swamping it with obscure verbiage.

However that may be, the two hemispheres of our brain are complementary as are reason and emotion, and Gestalt should be rightly credited for having reinstated the dignity of intuition which, for a while, had been overshadowed by the lightning breakthrough of scientism in the past century. The head without the body or the body without the head! Is this really the choice we are given ?

In fact, Perls was already fairly old when his method started to catch on and he himself hardly practiced "psychocorporal" Gestalt. Laura Perls, on the other hand, a musician and a dancer[6], constantly stressed that "bodily work is an integral part of Gestalt." She did not fear bodily contact, she willingly touched her clients and let them touch her.

Nowadays, practitioners differ according to their personalities, their philosophical and technical options and their initial training. Some confine themselves to verbal exchanges, merely evoking in words the client's bodily reactions; whereas others, influenced by a "neo-Reichian" tendency, sometimes utilize their own body and prompt their client to do likewise, giving expression to their emotions, even indeed experimenting with a tender or aggressive contact, in a "body to body therapy," considering that this kind of interaction mobilizes the brain's deep (limbic) strata, awakens archaic associations and favors the reorganization of mental images and of cognitive and affective representations. The mind is indeed no longer considered as being separate from the emotions, or from the body.

The discussion remains open on the advantages and limits of bodily involvement on the part of client and therapist. Obviously, the latter must be sure that he can control his own involvement and limit it strictly to what may benefit his client. The so-called "authenticity" of reactions should not be a pretext for erotic or aggressive personal satisfaction. The therapeutic work involving body is acceptable only when it remains within the limits of a rigorous professional code of ethics. There is a danger that excesses may harm the client's therapy as well as the therapist's social image and that of Gestalt as a whole (in this matter too often suspected of excessive liberalism).

On this point again, today's French Gestalt therapists clearly distinguish themselves from Perls' practices. (Perls willingly engaged in sexual intercourse, sustained both by his own drives and by his need to provoke the establishment of his time).

18. Aggression

Perls, as well as Lorenz and many others, considered both aggression and sexuality as a "life drive,". He advocated one and the other as basic libidinal values allowing the survival of the individual and the species.

For him as for Melanie Klein, they are archaic drives which appear right from the oral stage. As soon as he has teeth, the infant starts biting, and it is through aggression that he assimilates his environment: the air he breathes, the food he chews, "destroys," swallows and then digests. As is well known, this theme of oral aggression has been one of the pretexts for Perls' quarrel with Freud, who himself linked aggression to anality, and then to the death instinct. Today, Gestalt therapists have still not really disavowed their master on this point: many are those who, following in the footsteps of ethologists (Lorenz, Montagnier, etc.), always emphasize *vital aggression* and do not hesitate to use provocation and confrontation to mobilize the client's energetic resources. In this way they avoid both mothering and alienating overprotection and excessive or lasting frustration—which might discourage the patient and fix him in a feeling of abandonment or of passiveness.

Accordingly, we stick to the term's etymology, since *ad-gressere* (going and meeting the other) as well as *pro-gressere* (going forward) contrast with *re-gressere* (going backward).

19. Creativity and imagination

Finally most basic principles of Gestalt therapy focus on the liberty of being oneself and of expressing oneself freely in an active and creative form, letting the right side of the brain speak symbolic and metaphorical language—a primitive language inherited from our distant ancestors, phylogenetic Esperanto made up of mental hieroglyphs. The therapist is an interpreter of the symbolic who thus opposes "diabolic" forces: he expresses himself not in a scientific and "mathematic" language, but in artistic and "poetic" language[7].

From the outset, the creative aspect of Gestalt Therapy has been emphasized by its precursors and pioneers (Otto Rank, Goodman, Zinker, etc.) and has not faded away since. Gestalt Therapy has always taken pride of being more of an art than a science.

20. The individual in the group

The extent of the value placed on the existential originality and creativity of each human being is best seen when one is confronted with others: it stands out fully at the point where the individual meets his environment. When practiced in therapeutic groups, Gestalt Therapy aims not at integrating the individual in a social sub-group, but rather at enabling him to better define his specificity. Gestalt Therapy therefore does not become a *group therapy*, but rather an *individual therapy within a group*. The participants are witnesses for each other's individual work: they generally intervene only on the therapist's or client's request, and during an eventual "feed-back" time. They talk about themselves—not about the interpretation they make of others. The group serves then as a sort of better "resonance chamber" for each participant's problems. The group helps both to define problems more clearly and to make them less dramatic.

Perls was an unstable and troubled creative genius. He hardly ever carried through any successful deep therapy over a long period of time, especially after he had left New York, at the age of 63, when he started a long wandering life which was to last 14 years. He traveled throughout the United States and the world trying to sell his method by means of lectures and demonstrations. He therefore gradually abandoned the notion of a thorough individual psychotherapy in favor of therapeutic groups—even for the large public on a periodic and short term basis. Toward the end of his life, consistent with his own practice, he seems to have overvalued group therapies, placing them above individual therapies; later on he did the same with community therapy (through "Gestalt-Kibbutz"), which he briefly tried to set up when he retired in Cowichan, in Vancouver Island, but this experience was ended a few months later when he died on March 14, 1970.

Thirty five years later most present-day French practitioners combine several types of activity:

- individual *one-to-one* therapy (generally once a week over a period of several years)
- individual therapy *in groups* (for example, one evening each week or a week-end each month, over a period of one or two years).
- Both therapeutic approaches are often combined and reinforce each other—particularly when they are used by the same therapist, thus thwarting the eventual avoidances of the client.
- but, recalling that "Gestalt is too good to be restricted to ill persons" (Perls), several practitioners also organize limited personal resources' development groups (for example, 3 to 5 days once or several times a year). Some others use Gestalt Therapy as a secondary method in a psychological, educational or social practice (for example in institutions for maladjusted children or in psychiatric hospitals, and even in commercial or industrial firms, as trainers or consultants).

Conclusion

Although Perls' peculiar genius has decidedly marked the development of Gestalt Therapy, we must not forget the important contributions of his first collaborators: Laura Perls, Paul Goodman, Isadore From, Jim Simkin, Erv and Miriam Polster, Joseph Zinker, etc.

Thirty five years after his death, Perls' personal influence remains on several points: awareness, development, the holistic approach, the notion of homeostasis, the therapist "controlled involvement", provocative interventions, the status of aggression, the interest in the richness of the group situation, etc.

On the other hand, todays's French practitioners have distanced themselves from many attitudes or habits of the founder. Unlike Perls, they supplement and deepen theoretical research; they take into account the unconscious phenomena and transferential mechanisms; they rarely use the "hot seat" technique and the various games and exercises of Perls' time; they do not seek emotional catharsis (they just accompany it when it occurs spontaneously); they scrupulously respect the deontological rules of psychotherapy.

Thus, a specific French Gestalt Therapy is gradually taking shape, bringing a consistent synthesis between a local culture impregnated with psychoanalysis and mobilizing contributions of a more interactive method which emphasizes the contact cycle and its fluctuations, which brings back into favor emotion, body and the right side of the brain. Some observers underline that for the past 30 years or so, Gestalt therapy, once again nourished by its European roots, has been developing with more vigor and creativity on the continent of its founder.

Let us hope that in thirty years, Gestalt will remain at the forefront of humanistic therapies, without becoming fossilized, and that it will always show itself capable of integrating the continuous advances of research in psychology, biology and sociology.

Notes

1. This article has been first printed in the French national Gestalt Journal, called *Gestalt*, issue n°1 (Fall 1990).
2. *Translator's note:* reference to the 'Revolution' of May 1968 in France and in Paris in particular. Demonstrations by students and general strike

brought down the government. May 1968 marked a water-shed in French social and political life.

3. Translator's note: *Resistance* here refers to the underground movement during the German occupation of France in World War II.

4. Expression often mistakingly ascribed to Sartre, who in fact had declared—in a quite different context: «As a questioning on praxis, philosophy is at the same time a questioning on man. The main thing is not what has been done with man, but what he has done with what has been done with him. What has been done with man are the structures, the [. . .] studied by the social sciences. What he has made is history itself. Philosophy stands between the two» (Interview in *L'Arc*, oct. 1966).

5. Variation of the Psychodrama, borrowed from Moreno, in which the client himself plays different roles alternatively.

6. Parallel to her gestaltist and psychoanalytic formation, Laura Perls had followed various "psychocorporal" training programs (Alexander Method, Feldenkrais Method, etc.)

7. "Sym-bolic, " from sun-bolein (to throw together) is opposed to "dia-bolic," from dia-bolein (to throw apart to separate). "Poetic," from poiein (to create) is opposed to "mathematics", from mathema (learned by heart, to repeat what one already knows).

Annexes

Glossary

Short bibliography

Practical information

Glossary

Some technical terms have been already defined in the chapters 4 (Theory of the Self) and 11 (Twenty basic notions)

acting out: cf. *enactment*

aggression: (from the Latin *ad-gredere*, to go towards the other; opposite *re-gredere*, to draw back, to go backwards; similar to *pro-gredere*, to progress, to go forward). For Perls, as for contemporary ethologists, aggression is a *life* instinct and not a 'death instinct', as it was for Freud; necessary for the active assimilation of the external world in order to avoid introjections: first you have to bite the apple and chew it (destroy it) before you can digest it. The same for ideas, before to adopt them.

amplification: classical Gestalt technique consisting of encouraging the client to amplify their unconscious gestures, sensations or spontaneous feelings, in order to make them more explicit and in order for the client to become more aware of them.

assertiveness: realistic self affirmation, without bragging or false modesty. Defense of one's own interests or point of view, without denying those of others.

avoidance (mechanism): an expression synonymous with "defense mechanism", or "loss of ego function" or again, "resistance".

awareness: global awareness in the 'now', giving attention to the whole of one's physical sensations and feelings, both internal and environmental (awareness of oneself and of what one perceives outside oneself), as well as of one's thought processes.

awareness continuum: the ongoing *flow* of sensations, feelings and thoughts which makes up the *ground* from which the main *figures* (*Gestalts* or *Gestalten*) of our interest emerge. In someone who is psychologically healthy, this flow is flexible and uninterrupted.

bullshit: colloquial expression, used freely by Perls, to denounce intellectualizing. He distinguished between *"chickenshit"*, *"bullshit"* and *"elephant shit"* . . . depending on the extent of these defensive intellectual games, rationalizations or long verbalizations,—which he believed were generally unproductive. In an over-reaction to psychoanalysis, he dismissed all theorizing.

catharsis: the sometimes spectacular expression of an emotion, (anger, shouts, sobs), enabling a possible *abreaction*, release or dedramatisation. In Gestalt, catharsis is not pursued as an end in itself, but often occurs as a result of *amplification*. It is almost always followed by a verbal account.

Cleveland: one of the main Gestalt Institutes in the United States. The second to have been set up (1954); one of the most influential in terms of theory. The faculty comprised among others, Laura Perls, P. Goodman, I. From, E. and M Polster, J. Zinker, E. and S. Nevis, etc. To date, the Institute of Cleveland has trained more than 1000 people (half of them in an intensive summer program of 250 hours).

client: "a person who has recourse to someone's services, in return for payment". This term is not used exclusively in business relationships. It is currently used in the social services and in psychotherapy: it has a more *interactive* and less medical connotation than *patient*, (a person who suffers or receives treatment, with a certain *passivity*).

concentration: when Perls first started practicing (in the '40s and '50s), he called his approach *Concentration Therapy* to distinguish it from traditional psychoanalysis which advocated *free association*. He suggested that the client pay particular attention (*awareness*) to what s/he was feeling in the *here and now* of the therapy session.

confluence: diminution of the *self*, abolition of the *boundary* between the client and his/her environment. One of the four classical *resistances*. A mother and her baby are in *healthy confluence*, but a 12-year-old child who is unable to take a different stance from his/her mother is suffering from unhealthy confluence. Some writers identify different sorts of confluence according to where on the cycle it occurs: *confluence 1*, when the need emerges; *confluence 2*, at the contact stage; *confluence 3*, at the end of the cycle (difficulty withdrawing).

contact: a central concept in Gestalt therapy. The normal *cycle* of needs satisfaction is often called the *contact cycle* (or *the cycle of contact and withdrawal*) . . . Therapy works at the contact boundary between the organism and its environment.

contact-boundary: a basic concept in Gestalt. The therapy takes place at the *contact-boundary* between the client and his/her environment (in particular, the therapist); the place where interruptions to contact (or *resistances*) and to the normal cycle of needs satisfaction are found. The *skin* is an example and above all a metaphor for the contact boundary: it separates me and connects me at the same time.

contact cycle: fundamental concept in Gestalt, developed by Goodman in his *Theory of the Self*. He distinguishes *four main stages* to every action: fore-contact, contacting, final contact, post-contact (or withdrawal). This cycle has been developed and amended by various writers, notably Zinker, Polster, Katzeff, Smith, Salathe, Ginger, etc. Katzeff identifies seven stages: sensation, awareness, mobilization, action, contact, satisfaction, withdrawal.

Ginger identifies *five*: forecontact, engagement, contact, disengagement, assimilation.

Interruptions or disturbances to the natural progresssion round the cycle are often called 'resistances'.

controlled involvement: an attitude of conscious involvement in the therapeutic relationship, advocated in Gestalt and implying a careful exploration of the *counter transference*. I am here *myself*, fully, as a whole and authentic person; however, I am not here *for* myself, but for the client.

counter-transference: in the narrow sense, the *therapist's* conscious and above all unconscious *responses* induced by the person of the client (and notably by his/her *transference*). In a *wider* sense, *everything* which, from *the person of the therapist*, can impact on the relationship. Gestalt consciously exploits some counter-transferential processes.

Cowichan: at the end of 1969, Perls, then aged 76, bought a fishermen's motel at the edge of Lake Cowichan on Vancouver Island (Canada) and with a small group of disciples from Esalen, founded a *Gestalt-kibbutz*. He lived there for six months, before leaving on a trip to Europe, and died in Chicago on the way back.

creative adjustment: term first used by Goodman to describe the active interaction (not passive adaptation) that occurs at the *contact boundary* between a healthy person and their environment.

deflection: one of the 'resistances' or 'losses of ego function' (identified by the Polsters). Deflection consists of avoiding contact by rerouting the feeling towards an *'intermediate zone'* of *mental processes*, (ideas, fantasies or daydreams), which is neither external reality nor the reality perceived by my internal being. It may therefore be an *escape from the here and now* into memories, plans, abstract thinking, etc. into what Perls thought of as "*mind fucking*" or "*bullshit*".

dream: the 'royal road' to self knowledge, for *Perls* as for Freud. Taking Rank's idea, Perls considered every person or element in the dream as a *projection* of the dreamer and often suggested embodying them in turn. Other writers suggest thinking of the dream as *retroflection* (I. From) or as an *unfinished Gestalt* (Ginger). A combination of these various approaches often proves worthwhile.

EAGT: European Association for Gestalt Therapy, founded in 1985. Conferences: Germany in '86, Netherlands in '89, France (Paris) in '92, Great Britain (Cambridge) in '95, Italy (Palerma) in 1998, Sweden (Stokholm) in 2001, Czech Republic (Prague) in 2004, Greece (Athens) in 2007.

Ego: the *self* can function in three ways, as the *Id*, the *Ego*, the *Personality*. The *Ego* is an active function, implying awareness of my needs and taking responsibility for my choices. *Losses of ego function* are often called "resistances".

egotism: a 'resistance' with a rather specific meaning, as defined by Goodman. Artificial over-expansion of the *ego*, which aims to encourage narcissism and the taking of personal responsibility, as a means of preparing for autonomy. It is thus a temporary therapeutic device. As with *transference neurosis* in psychoanalysis, this temporary phase must be worked through in the course of Gestalt therapy.

empathy: ability to identify with someone, to feel what they are feeling. Perls contrasted *empathy*, defined by C. Rogers, with *sympathy* where the therapist allows him/herself to exist fully, so as to offer the client a partner, with an authentic 'I/thou' relationship in mind.

enactment: the conscious enacting of a situation, followed by a verbal exploration, allowing the client to see a phenomenon more clearly, and to make *explicit* what is implicit. The enactment is *different from impulsive 'acting out'* which short-circuits verbal awareness, by substituting an acted outburst which is difficult to analyze.

Esalen institute: located in Big Sur (California), 300 km to the South of San Francisco, considered to have been the most famous Center in the world for the so-called "humanistic, new therapies". Perls stayed there several years, building a reputation for Gestalt, and transforming it in the process into something of a 'show'.

experiment: Gestalt is an existential and experiential approach, which advocates living, testing out, feeling, experiencing or consciously experimenting for oneself (often in the first place at the *symbolic* level) with feared or hoped-for situations.

feedback: a regulatory reaction in response to a situation. In group therapy, participants are often asked to give a client feedback at the end of a particular piece of work. The aim may be to provide additional information to help the *client* in question become more fully aware, but feedback most often concerns *the person who gives it*, encouraging him/her to express their own feelings, i.e. the personal resonances experienced as a result of the situation, preparing the way in due course for a piece of work of his own.

figure/ground: basic concept in Gestalt *psychology* (or Theory of Form), developed further in Gestalt therapy. A healthy person must be able to discern clearly and with immediacy the current *dominant figure* (or *Gestalt*) which only assumes its full meaning in relation to the *'ground'*, the background. So, a reaction in the here-and-now (emerging figure) must fit into the 'whole' of situation and personality (ground). [cf. *awareness continuum*]

FORGE: *Federation Internationale des Organismes de Formation à la Gestalt*, International Federation of Gestalt Training Organizations. Founded in 1991.
Gathers 30 training institutes from 20 countries.
183, rue Lecourbe, 75015 Paris. France.
Fax: + 33 1 53 68 64 57. E-mail: ginger@noos.fr
Elected Board: President: S. Ginger (France), Vice-Presidents: Sergio Vazquez (Mexico), G. Skottun (Norway), General Secretary: N. Lebedeva (Russia), Treasurer: G. Masquelier (France); Members

of the Board: A. Ravenna (Italy), G. Delisle (Canada), J. van Pevenage (Belgium).

Exchange of ideas, programs, documents, trainers and trainees. Approval of international programs.

Colloquium every year in a different country.

form (and content): Gestalt underlines the importance of *process* and manner; the often unaware or unconscious *way* in which something is said or done, (the *how* of intonation, expressions, posture, gesture, etc.) which enriches or contradicts the intended *content* of what is *said* or *done.*

Gestalt psychology or *Gestalt theory*, or the *Theory of Form*: Psychological movement, inspired by phenomenology, dating from 1912 (Ehrenfels, Wertheimer, Koffka, Koehler), which emphasizes that "the whole is different from the sum of all the parts", and is the result of the many interactions of the parts on each other. Brings to light the subjective nature of perception.

GT: common abbreviation for *Gestalt Therapy.*

here-and-now: Perls speaks more readily of the *now and how,* describing the on-going *process* of the action or interaction.

holism, holistic: from the Greek *'holos',* the whole; pertaining to the whole. Perls was profoundly influenced by the holistic theory of J.C. Smuts, the Prime Minister of South Africa, one of the forces behind the *League of Nations,* who in 1926 published *Holism and Evolution,* drawing on the ideas of Darwin, Bergson, Einstein and Teilhard de Chardin.

homeostasis: general principle of the *self-regulations of living organisms,* defined by Cannon in 1926. Perls stresses this idea, notably in his posthumous work *The Gestalt approach and Eye Witness to Therapy,* which he began in 1950, completed in 1970, and which was published in 1973, after his death.

hot seat: a technique that Perls was particularly fond of, (especially after 1964, during his 'Californian period'), which consists of inviting the client to come and sit on a chair near the therapist (the hot seat), most of the time facing an *empty chair*—on which s/he can imagine and speak to a particular person, (e.g. his/her father). This seat can also be represented by a cushion or any other object.

how: from a basic *phenomenological* perspective, Gestalt is more concerned with the *how* than with the *what* or the *why,* i.e. Gestalt concerns itself above all with the *process* and the *way in which something is expressed*, the *manner* as much as the *content* . . . Two key words in Gestalt are *"now and how"*.

Humanistic Psychology: term introduced by A. Maslow (1954): 'the Third Force'; a movement which reacted against the all-pervading, hierarchical *determinism* of *psychoanalysis* on the one hand, and *behaviorism* on the other. From an existential point of view, humanistic psychology aims to give back to the individual full *responsibility* for his/her choices and to reinstate his/her spiritual *values*.

hyperventilation: a technique of forced breathing, amplified and/or speeded up, used particularly in *bioenergetics*, in *rebirthing* and in *holotropic breathing* (Grof), and aiming to free up the subcortical (limbic) layers by 'intoxicating' the cortical control through hyper oxygenation. Freeing up buried emotions often provokes catharsis, which may be accompanied by convulsive movements or spasms. In Gestalt, this kind of *artificial* technique is not used, but sometimes *spontaneous* hyperventilation occurs, triggered by intense emotion.

Id: in the Gestalt sense, one of the three 'functions' of the *self*—which also consists of the *ego* and the *personality*. The *self* generally functions in the *id* mode at the beginning of the *cycle*, during the so-called *precontact* (or *forecontact*) phase. For certain writers, assimilation (postcontact) also takes place, outside of awareness, in the *id* mode.

impasse: term used by Perls to indicate a situation of blocked psychological energy, with no apparent way out, suggesting this may be the root of the problem.

insight, satori: a sudden awareness, an 'aha', resulting from a strong internal experience.

introjection: one of the classic 'resistances', consisting of swallowing whole the ideas or values of others, without digesting and assimilating them in one's own way. It is particularly concerned with the 'shoulds and oughts' of traditional education.

isism: a word derived from the English *'what is'* and coined by Perls to denote a realistic vision of what *exists*, as opposed to my imaginary desires or fears. The opposite is *shouldism*, what should be, what I would wish to be the case.

I/thou: alludes to the work of Buber (*I and Thou*, 1923); expresses the direct, authentic person-to-person relationship (*sympathy*) advocated by Perls, including that of the therapy session.

kibbutz-group: the application of Gestalt principles in a medium- or long-term residential community setting, lasting from a few days to a few months. The actual therapeutic work alternates with a shared life of work, study or leisure, giving rise to a shared therapeutic experience. In the early days, Perls favored *individual* therapy, then *group* therapy, and ultimately, *community* therapy (cf. Cowichan).

loss of ego function: an expression synonymous with "resistance", "defense mechanism", avoidance mechanism, interruption of the cycle, etc. Each writer adopts their own terminology. (cf. *resistance*)

mandala: Sanskrit word meaning "circle". A *symbolic drawing (or painting)*, generally in the form of a circle or square, used by various Eastern philosophies as a meditation aid, in the search for inner truth. C.G. Jung made a particular study of *mandalas*. The visual, symbolic representation of feelings or situations and various techniques inspired by the *mandala* are currently used by some Gestaltists.

mental shuttle: moving to-and-fro between the (socially observable) *external* reality and *inner reality* (what the client experiences phenomenologically or in fantasy), between feeling and verbal awareness, between the client's everyday life and the metaphorical situation represented in the here-and-now of the session, between the present and the past, etc. The *shuttle* is widely used in Gestalt.

metaphor: metaphoric language—verbal, bodily, artistic—is widely used in Gestalt.

micro-gestures: small, automatic gestures, most of which are out of awareness or unconscious (e.g. finger tapping, foot tapping, occasional 'tics' or facial expressions, playing with a ring, etc.)

Becoming aware of, then *amplifying* such gestures often enables the client to discover for him/herself their *symbolic* meaning, opening up rich *paths of association*.

middle mode: for Goodman, and with reference to Greek grammar, the mood both *active and passive* of the functioning of the *self*, particularly noticeable at the so-called 'full contact' stage, which is both motor and sensory. The client is both the *subject and the object* of his/her action.

monodrama: a psychodrama technique invented by Moreno and often used by Perls, consisting of getting the *client* to play in turn the various roles of the situation s/he is recalling. In this way, s/he can dialogue, for example, with various parts of his/her own body, or open up an imaginary dialogue with one of his/her parents and give the responses that s/he him/herself imagines, fears or desires. (In this way, s/he dialogues with his/her parental *imago*.)

needs: in Gestalt, one is more interested in *needs* than in *wishes*. Needs may be organic (to eat, sleep . . .), psychological, social or spiritual: the need to be included in a group, the need to find a meaning in life, etc. (Maslow). They are not necessarily either clearly perceived or directly expressed. The *'cycle of needs satisfaction'* is often interrupted or disturbed and one of the aims of Gestalt work is to identify these interruptions, blocks or distortions. (cf. *'resistances'*)

now and how: two of the four key words in Gestalt ("Now and how; I and thou"), which encapsulate the full and authentic relationship between two people, in the here and now of the therapy session.

'Perls' prayer': a famous and frequently quoted denouncement of *confluence*.

Personality: see *Ego*. The *personality function* of the *self* is the way the client represents her/himself using words, the *self image* by which s/he recognizes him/herself. It therefore has the function of *integrating* experience, which is the basis of the sense of identity, into a reality of its own. It is particularly evident at the *end of the contact cycle*, when the current experience is ending, at the moment of *withdrawal* (assimilating the experience which will enrich my *personality*).

personal style: Gestalt presents itself as an *art* rather than a science and encourages both client and therapist to find their own personal ways of being in the world, to make their own individual 'creative adjustments' and not seek vainly to apply rigid rules or formulae.

physical sensation: awareness of *exteroceptive* or *interoceptive* physical sensation (e.g. a feeling of heaviness, a knot in the stomach, a lump in the throat, etc.) is often used as the *starting point* for deeper work. The therapist, on his/her side, also stays *attentive to his/her own physical sensations*. This allows him/her to be aware of and to be informed by her/his counter-transference in the service of the client.

polarities: Gestalt seeks the harmonious *integration* of all the complementary *polarities* of human behavior (e.g. aggression and tenderness) rather than the elimination of one at the expense of the other or the illusory search for an 'unhappy' medium, the pale greyness of dulled feelings.

post-contact or 'withdrawal': the fourth and final stage of *the contact cycle* or the cycle of need satisfaction according to Goodman; the essential stage of *assimilation*, which feeds the *personality function*.

precontact (or forecontact): the first stage of Goodman's *contact-withdrawal* cycle. The *self* functions primarily in the *id* mode (sensation, excitement). *Precontact* is often disturbed, even absent, in psychotics.

process: Gestalt is primarily a therapy which focuses on *process* rather than on content, on what is happening in the here-and-now, on the *how* and not on the *what*.

proflection: a term recently introduced by Sylvia Crocker to describe a composite from of 'resistance' which links *projection* with *retroflection*. It consists of doing to others what we would like others to do to us.

projection: a classic form of 'resistance' which consists of attributing to others what belongs to oneself. A resistance particularly marked among paranoids.

proxemics: the scientific study of the organization of social space and *social distances*, (Edward Hall, 1966). Finding the 'right distance' in relationship is an ongoing theme in Gestalt.

resistance: a fundamental concept in Gestalt, mainly concerned with identifying the 'resistances' which prevent free movement round the *cycles of contact or needs satisfaction*, and the unfolding of the self. The main classical *resistances* are: confluence, introjection, projection and retroflection. Some authors add deflection, proflexion, egotism, invalidation, etc.

retroflection: turning back against oneself mobilized energy (e.g. masochism or somatization) or doing to oneself what one would like others to do to us (e.g. boasting). Retroflection may express the internal struggle between top-dog and under-dog.

self: in Gestalt, this word does not denote a well-defined entity (unlike, for example, the *ego*, in Psychoanalysis), but a *process*: what happens at the *contact boundary* between the organism and its environment, enabling *creative adjustments* to occur. So, in certain circumstances, (e.g. in moments of confluence), the self may diminish. Goodman elaborated *The Theory of the Self* (ch. 8) in 1951, working from Perls' notes.

SGM: Sensitive Gestalt Massage, (developed by the American, Margaret Elke), closely related to Californian style massage, sensory, relaxing, relational, etc. A technique of non-verbal communication focusing on the physical awareness of the two partners who, in turn, both give and receive massage. Among its aims, the *reintegration* of a physical sense of self—a good way to heighten awareness at the *contact boundary*.

setting: the surroundings, the material conditions of a therapy session: face to face, couch, etc. The setting may vary depending on the *method* used, the *therapist*, the *client* and the *point reached* in the therapeutic journey. It plays an important part in the development of any therapy—a fact which is often not sufficiently recognized either by the client or by some therapists.

shouldism: a word coined by Perls, (from the English *'should'*, as in *'it should be so'*) to describe the attitude of those who deny reality by escaping into fantasy.

socio-Gestalt: an expression used by S. Ginger to designate a branch of Gestalt applied to institutions or organizations taken *as a whole.* (It refers to the Gestalt *of* the organization and not Gestalt *in* the organization.)

stress: internal, psychological pressure, either positive or negative, connected most frequently to a painful, external event (conflict, grief, etc.), but also to any situation entailing significant life changes (marriage, holidays, etc.). Basing their work on that of Selye (1956), Holmes and Rahe drew up a *scale of stressors* (1967). The accumulation of stress weakens the defenses of the immune system and favors the appearance of illness (cancer, etc.) The expression of emotions—advocated by Gestalt Therapy—lessens tensions and stress.

sympathy: For Perls, *sympathy* is distinct from *empathy* and *apathy.* *Sympathy* presupposes the therapist's authentic involvement in the 'I/thou' person-to-person relationship, without hiding behind a role.

systemic: the systemic approach (von Bertalanffy, 1956; Goldstein, Le Moigne, de Rosnay, Morin) is distinct from the rationalist, Newtonian-Cartesian approach in that it sees every problem as a 'collection of wholes in interaction with one another'. Gestalt is a systemic approach which explores the *interactions* in the organism/environment *field*. This approach is put to further psychotherapeutic use in *systemic family therapy*, (Palo Alto school: Bateson, Watzlawick).

top-dog: literally, the dog leading a team of sledges. By extension, the boss or leader, notably in sports. Perls emphasizes the intrapsychic struggle between the top-dog (conscience, *super ego*) and the under-dog ("second fiddle", *egotistic* resistance).

transference: in psychoanalysis, the intense affective relationship which develops between the client and the therapist, and to some extent, recreates an attitude lived out during childhood: *transference neurosis* is the main force behind cure. In Gestalt, many *spontaneous* transferential phenomena can, of course, be found. These are explored *as they occur*. The therapist does not artificially develop *transference neurosis* which creates a dependence on the therapist.

transitional object: in Winnicott, an object invested with feelings by the child and used as *a mother substitute*, which has a self-calming function (e.g. a soft toy or the corner of a blanket or pillow). In the *wider sense* (used in Gestalt), an object symbolizing an absent person to which one is attached.

transitional space: cf. *transitional object*. Transitional *space* (Winnicott) is the space for play, art or therapy—midway between reality and fantasy.

transpersonal: therapy can be *intrapersonal* (analysis of internal conflicts), *interpersonal* (study of relationships established between people) or *transpersonal* (taking into account the collective unconscious and the esoteric ties which link the human race with the cosmos). Gestalt favors any one of these dimensions or all three at once,—depending on the individual style of the therapist and the particular needs of the client.

unconscious: in Gestalt, the importance of unconscious phenomena is not denied, but they are not the main focus of the therapeutic work. Gestalt therapy deliberately starts at the surface with observable bodily, emotional or mental phenomena, in order to reach the deeper *unconscious* layers.

unfinished (business, situation, Gestalt): the accumulation of *unfinished Gestalts* would, according to Perls, be one of the causes of neurosis. Therapy will therefore consist mainly of closing *unfinished* or *fixed* Gestalts, i.e. of working on areas that have been left unresolved, (e.g. grieving).

voice: work with the voice is essential in Gestalt, where the *way* in which something is said is as important as *what* is said. A voice which is stifled, delivered in short bursts or without intonation may be evidence of a state of mind which is different from what the client is expressing verbally, thus providing an often fruitful path for exploration. *Assertive* self affirmation (genuine self-confidence, without boasting) is used in Gestalt groups.

withdrawal or 'post-contact': the fourth and final stage of the *contact cycle* according to Goodman, which enables an experience to be assimilated, (*personality function of the self*), and creates the sense of *identity*. Too brutal or slow (*confluence*) a withdrawal is a sign of dysfunction, which hinders the development of autonomy.

Zeigarnik effect: the mobilizing mental pressure which arises from the vague feeling of *an unfinished task to be completed*. Studied by Bluma Zeigarnik. Used in education and in advertising (to keep people's interest alive). But according to Perls, the *excessive* repetition of incomplete 'Gestalts' is a cause of neurosis.

Short Glossary English/French

ENGLISH	FRANÇAIS	ENGLISH	FRANÇAIS
acting out	passage à l'acte	hyperventilation	hyperventilation
aggression	agressivité	I/Thou	je/tu
amplification	amplification	id	ça
assertiveness	assertivité	impasse	impasse
avoidance	évitement	implosion	implosion
awareness	*awareness*	introjection	introjection
awareness continuum	continuum de conscience	loss of ego function	perte de la fonction ego
body feeling	ressenti corporel	metaphor	métaphore
catharsis	catharsis	micro-movement	micro-geste
character	caractère	middle mode	mode moyen
client	client	monodrama	monodrame
concentration	concentration	needs	besoins
confluence	confluence	now and how	*now and how*
contact	contact	personal style	style personnel
contact cycle	cycle de contact	personality	personnalité
contact functions	fonctions de contact	polarities	polarités
contact boundary	frontière-contact	post-contact	post-contact
controlled involvment	implication contrôlée	process	processus
counter transference	contre-transfert	proflection	proflexion
creative adjustment	ajustement créateur	projection	projection
deflection	déflexion	proxemics	proxémique
disengagement	désengagement	resistances	résistances
dream	rêve	retroflection	rétroflexion
ego	moi	self	*self*
egotism	égotisme	setting	*setting*
enactment	mise en action	shuttle	navette mentale
engagement	engagement	socio-Gestalt	socio-Gestalt
experiment	expérimentation	stress	stress
fantasy	rêverie-éveillée	sympathy	sympathie
feedback	*feed-back*	systemic	systémique
figure/ground	figure/fond	training	formation
fore-contact	pré-contact	transference	transfert
form	forme	transitional	transitionnel
general semantics	sémantique générale	transitional object	objet transitionnel
Gestalt prayer	prière de Perls	transpersonal	transpersonnel
Gestalt-psychology	Gestalt-psychologie	unconscious	inconscient
here and now	ici et maintenant	unfinished (business)	inachevé (travail, Gestalt)
holism	holisme	unfinished business	situation inachevée
homeostasis	homéostasie	voice	voix
how	comment	withdrawal	retrait
Humanistic Psychology	psychologie humaniste	Zeigarnik effect	effet Zeigarnik

Short Glossary French/English

FRANÇAIS	ENGLISH	FRANÇAIS	ENGLISH
agressivité	aggression	je/tu	I/Thou
ajustement créateur	creative adjustment	métaphore	metaphor
amplification	amplification	micro-geste	micro-movement
assertivité	assertiveness	mise en action	enactment
awareness	awareness	mode moyen	middle mode
besoins	needs	moi	ego
ça	*id*	monodrame	monodrama
caractère	character	navette mentale	shuttle
catharsis	catharsis	*now and how*	now and how
client	client	objet transitionnel	transitional object
comment	how	passage à l'acte	acting out
concentration	concentration	personnalité	personality
confluence	confluence	perte de la fonction ego	loss of ego function
contact	contact	polarités	polarities
continuum de conscience	awareness continuum	post-contact	post-contact
contre-transfert	counter transference	pré-contact	fore-contact
cycle de contact	contact cycle	prière de Perls	Gestalt prayer
déflexion	deflection	processus	process
désengagement	disengagement	proflexion	proflection
effet Zeigarnik	Zeigarnik effect	projection	projection
égotisme	egotism	proxémique	proxemics
engagement	engagement	psychologie humaniste	Humanistic Psychology
évitement	avoidance	résistances	resistances
expérimentation	experiment	ressenti corporel	body feeling
feed-back	feedback	retrait	withdrawal
figure/fond	figure/ground	rétroflexion	retroflection
fonctions de contact	contact functions	rêve	dream
formation	training	rêverie-éveillée	fantasy
forme	form	*self*	self
frontière-contact	contact boundary	sémantique générale	general semantics
Gestalt-psychologie	Gestalt-psychology	*setting*	setting
holisme	holism	situation inachevée	unfinished business
homéostasie	homeostasis	socio-Gestalt	*socio-Gestalt*
hyperventilation	hyperventilation	stress	stress
ici et maintenant	here and now	style personnel	personal style
impasse	impasse	sympathie	sympathy
implication contrôlée	controlled involvment	systémique	systemic
implosion	implosion	transfert	transference
inachevé (travail, Gestalt)	unfinished (business)	transitionnel	transitional
inconscient	unconscious	transpersonnel	transpersonal
introjection	introjection	voix	voice

Short bibliography

in English

CLARKSON P. (1989). *Gestalt counselling in action.* London. Sage.

CLARKSON P. & MACKEWN J. (1993). *Fritz Perls.* London. Sage.

CLARKSON P. (1995). *The therapeutic relationship.* London. Whurr.

ENRIGHT J. (1980). *Enlightening Gestalt.* Mill Valley. Pro Telos.

ERSKINE R. & MOURSUND J. (1988). *Integrative Psychotherapy in action.* London. Sage.

FAGAN J. & SHEPHERD I. (1970). *Gestalt Therapy now.* New-York. Harper & Row.

FAGAN J. & SHEPHERD I. (1970). *What is Gestalt?* New York. Harper & Row.

FEDER B. & RONALL R. (1980). *Beyond the Hot Seat.* New York. Brunner/ Mazel.

GAINES J. (1979). *Fritz Perls Here and Now.* Milbrae. Celestial Arts.

GINGER S. & al. (1995). *International Glossary of Gestalt Therapy.* Paris, FORGE.

GOODMAN P. (1977). *Native Heals. Psychological Essays.* New York. Free Life.

HATCHER C. & HIMELSTEIN P. (1976). *The Handbook of Gestalt Therapy.* New York. Aronson.

HYCNER R. & JACOBS L. *The Healing Relationship* in *Gestalt Therapy.* N.Y. GT. Journal.

KEMPLER W. (1972). *Principles of Gestalt Family Therapy.* Salt Lake City. Desert Press.

KEPNER J. (1987). *Body Process, a Gestalt Approach to Working with the Body in Psychotherapy.* NY. Gestalt Institute of Cleveland Press.

LATNER J. (1972). *The Gestalt Therapy Book.* New-York. Bantam Books.

LEVITSKY & PERLS. (1969). *Group therapy today: styles, methods and techniques.* Atherton.

142

MASQUELIER G. (2006). *Gestalt Therapy: living creatively Today*. Santa Cruz, CA. Gestalt Press.

MILLER M. V. (1995). *Intimate Terrorism: the Deterioration of Erotic Life*. N.Y. GT. Journal.

NARANJO C. (1973). *The Techniques of Gestalt Therapy*. Berkeley. SAT. Press.

NARANJO C. (1993). *Gestalt Therapy: the attitude and practice of an atheoritical experientialism*. Nevada Gateways.

NEVIS E. (1988). *Organizational consulting: a Gestalt Approach*. New York. Cleveland Press.

OAKLANDER V. (1978). *Windows to Our Children*. Moab. Real People Press.

PERLS F., HEFFERLINE R., GOODMAN P. (1951). *Gestalt Therapy*. New-York. Julian Press.

PERLS F. (1942). *Ego, hunger and aggression: a revision of Freud's theory and method*. Durban, 42; London, 1947

PERLS F. (1969). *Gestalt Therapy Verbatim*. Moab. Real People Press.

PERLS F. (1969). *In and out the garbage pail*. La Fayette. Real People Press.

PERLS F. (1973). *The Gestalt Approach & Eye Witness to Therapy*. N.Y. Bantam Books.

PERLS F. (1975). *Legacy from Fritz*. Palo Alto. S & Behavior Books.

PERLS Laura. (1992). *Living at the Boundary*. Highland, NY. The Gestalt Journal.

POLSTER E. & M. (1973). *Gestalt Therapy integrated*. New York. Vintage Books.

POLSTER E. (1987). *Every Person's Life Is Worth A Novel*. Norton & Company. N.Y.

POLSTER E. (1995). *A Population of Selves*. San Francisco. Jossey-Bass.

POLSTER M. (1992). *Eve's Daughter, the Forbidden Heroism of Women*. New York. Gestalt Journal.

SHEPARD M. (1975). *). Fritz: an intimate portrait of Fritz Perls & Gestalt therapy*. N.Y. Saturday Review Press.

SIMKIN J. (1974). *Mini-lectures in Gestalt therapy*. Albany. Word Press.

SMITH E. (1976). *The growing edge of Gestalt Therapy*. N.Y. Brunner/Mazel.

SMUTS J.C. (1961). *Hollis and Evolution*. NY. Viking.

STEVENS B. (1970). *Don't Push the River*. Moab. Real People Press.

STEVENS J. (1971). *Awareness: exploring, experimenting, experiencing*. Real People Press.

STEVENS J. (1975). *Gestalt is*. New-York. Bantam Books.

STOEHR T. (1994). *Here, Now, Next: Paul Goodman and the Origins of Gestalt Therapy*. GIC

THE GESTALT JOURNAL: 2 volumes every year, since 1978, Highland. N.Y.

WHEELER G. (1991). *Gestalt reconsidered: a new approach to Contact and Resistance.* New York. Cleveland Press.

YONTEFF G. (1993). *Awareness, Dialogue & Process. Essays on Gestalt Therapy.* Gestalt Journal Press.

ZINKER J. (1977). *Creative process in Gestalt therapy.* N.Y. Brunner/Mazel.

ZINKER J. (1994). *In Search of Good Form. GT with Couples and Families.* San Francisco. Jossey-Bass.

Short bibliography

in French

(selection of some books)

CHANGEUX J.Pierre (1983). *L'homme neuronal*. Paris. Fayard, *420 p.*

DELACROIX Jean-Marie (2006). *La Troisième Histoire. Patient-psychothérapeute: fonds et formes du processus relationnel*, Dangles, St Jean de Braye, 480 p.

DELISLE Gilles (1991). *Les troubles de la personnalité, perspective gestaltiste*. Montréal. Le Reflet, *285 p.*

DELISLE Gilles (1998). *La relation d'objet en Gestalt- thérapie*. éd. du Reflet, Montréal, 390 p.

DELOURME Alain, MARC Edmond (2007). *La supervision en psychanalyse et en psychothérapie*. Dunod, Paris, *236 p.*

ELKAÏM Mony *et al.* (2003). *À quel psy se vouer?* Le Seuil, Paris, 460 p.

FERENCZI Sandor (1933). *Œuvres complètes* (4 tomes). Payot, Paris.

FREUD Sigmund (1900). *L'interprétation des rêves*. PUF, Paris.

GINGER Serge (1983). La Gestalt-thérapie [. . .] dans la pratique hospitalière *(p. 279–304)* in *Former à l'hôpital*, HONORÉ B., Toulouse, Privat, *350 p.*

GINGER Serge (1985). La Gestalt: une troisième voie ? *(p. 53–71)* in *Le Développement personnel et les Travailleurs sociaux,* sous la direction de VANOYE & GINGER, Paris, E.S.F., *145 p.*

GINGER Serge et Anne (1987). *La Gestalt, une thérapie du contact*. Paris, Hommes & Group., 7° éd. 2003, *540 p.*

GINGER Serge (1995). *La Gestalt, l'art du contact*. Marabout. Bruxelles; 9e éd. Paris, 2007, *290 p.*

GINGER Serge (1995). *Lexique international de Gestalt-thérapie (en 8 langues)*. éd. FORGE, Paris, *180 p.*

146   SHORT BIBLIOGRAPHY

GINGER Serge (2006). *Psychothérapie: 100 réponses pour en finir avec les idées reçues*, Dunod, Paris, 288 p.

GINGER S., MARC E., TARPINIAN A. *et al.* (2006). *Ête Psychothérapente Duhod*, Paris, 272 p.

JOUVET Michel (1992). *Le sommeil et le rêve.* Paris, Odile Jacob, 220 p.

JUNG Carl-Gustav (1962). *Ma vie.* Gallimard, Paris, 470 p.

JUSTON Didier (1990). *Le Transfert en psychanalyse et en Gestalt-thérapie.* Lille, La Boîte de Pandore, 290 p.

LABORIT Henri (1979). *L'inhibition de l'action.* Masson, Paris.

MARC Edmond (1988). *Guide pratique des Psychothérapies.* Paris. Retz. 1re éd. 82; 3e éd. 2000, 256 p.

MARTEL Brigitte (2004). *Sexualité, amour et Gestalt.* Paris. Interéditions, 175 p.

MASQUELIER Gonzague (1999). *Vouloir sa vie. La Gestalt-thérapie aujourd'hui.* Retz. Paris, 144 p.

NGUYEN Tan *et al.* (2005). *Pourquoi la psychothérapie?* Dunod, Paris, 308 p.

PERLS Fritz (1942). *Le Moi, la faim et l'agressivité.* Tchou, Paris, 1978.

PERLS Fritz (1969). *Rêves et existence en Gestalt-thérapie.* L'Épi, Paris.

PERLS Fritz. (1973). *Manuel de Gestalt-thérapie,* ESF, Paris, 2003, 128 p.; 2e édition: 2005. Préface de Ginger.

PERLS F., HEFFERLINE R., GOODMAN P. (1951). *Gestalt-thérapie.* Stanké, Montréal, 1979.

PETIT Marie. (1980). *La Gestalt, Thérapie de l'ici-maintenant,* Paris, 1e éd.: Retz,; 5e éd.: E.S.F., 1996, 184 p.

POLSTER Ervin & Miriam (1973). *La Gestalt : nouvelles perspectives.* Le Jour, Montréal, 1983.

ROBINE Jean-Marie (1998). *Gestalt-thérapie, la construction du soi,* L'Harmattan, Paris, 270 p.

SALATHÉ Noël (1992). *Psychothérapie existentielle.* Amers, Genève

VANOYE Francis, DELORY-MOMBERGER Christine (2005). *La Gestalt, thérapie du mouvement.* Vuibert, Paris, 250 p.

VINCENT J. Didier (1986). *Biologie des passions.* Paris. Seuil, 350 p.

ZINKER Joseph (1977). *La Gestalt-thérapie, un processus créatif.* InterEditions, Paris, 2006, 320 p. Traduction revue et corrigée. Préface de Ginger.

Practical information

(FAQ)

*Would you like to begin a therapy or develop your
personal resources?*

Perhaps you experience some difficulties in your life . . . some
personal suffering or various worries, current or long-term, oppress
you: fatigue, sadness, loneliness, grief over a death; excessive
shyness, anxiety, depression; hyper-activity, a lack of coherence
in your activities or interests; sexual or emotional difficulties;
problems with your children, your parents, your employer; problems
managing your money or food (anorexia, bulimia); physical or
psychosomatic illness; difficulties with an important decision; etc.

Or, more simply, you feel quite good in general, but you would
like to *use your potential to the maximum*: be more creative, more
adventurous, more serene, ground your spiritual search, develop
your understanding of yourself and others, enrich your special
relationship and your relationships in general, etc.

Or further, *your professional life involves human relationships*: special
education, social services, nurse, psychologist, doctor, teacher,
trainer, human resources director, minister, etc. and you would like
to deepen and refine your understanding and your availability to
others, by using the "Gestalt tool" adapted to your own personality,
or even *become a psychotherapist* yourself

. . . then Gestalt therapy can certainly help you!

How to go about it?
Where to begin?
Individual or group therapy?

If you are new to Gestalt Therapy and psychotherapy in general, you can attend a *lecture* (with or without a *demonstration*), or—better yet— a *short workshop* which will allow you to participate personally, as you wish, in several brief "work" sequences and understand more concretely the process of contact offered by Gestalt therapy.

For a more profound process of discovery or *development of your personal resources,* you are encouraged to participate in an *intensive workshop* lasting two or three days. Most of these workshops have no particular topic, and you may thus present those subjects which may concern you—in whatever area that may be—and thus try to achieve more clarity on the subject, with the help of the therapist/s who lead the group.

In these workshops, each participant expresses himself, in a personal way, *when he so desires,* for a variable period of time: from several minutes up to possibly an hour. Generally, the participant will begin by speaking and then will be invited to move about, to address someone in the group, to make a sketch, etc. You stay always *completely free* to accept or refuse any suggestion by the therapist. Each person works at his own rhythm and on the themes he has chosen himself. You may even remain silent and aloof during the session, "in your heart." Everything that is expressed in the group is protected by an agreement of a "shared secret" and this discretion is always well respected.

Of course, you may also consult a therapist individually—which may seem more simple and usual, as one would consult a doctor or a psychologist. Perhaps you would be more comfortable to share certain personal or intimate difficulties, in an atmosphere of confidentiality. The therapist will welcome you without judgment, in a direct and friendly way. He will listen to you with careful attention, yet will not stay closed within an intimidating silence.

He will express to you generally what he feels within himself in listening to you. He may propose a *series of interviews* to provide you comfort and moral support, or even perhaps a full-fledged *psychotherapy*—which would involve a regular commitment over a certain period: for example, one hour per week, during several months (*lasting from several months to two or three years, according to the need*). He may also suggest that you participate in a group therapy, which has often proved to be a precious help. Other people express their own concerns, often more or less close to our own, and we feel less alone, within a tolerant and friendly atmosphere, created by the Gestalt Therapist. Instead of feeling intimidated (which we may easily feel at first), we feel accepted, understood and we make some new friends. In fact, it is often easier to *begin* with group therapy rather than individual interviews, but that remains, of course, a personal choice.

The most interesting solution is to *combine the two approaches: individual* therapy (for example, one hour per week) + *group* therapy (for example, one evening each 15 days, or one week-end per month). But this requires a little more time . . . and money! However, the association of these two approaches (with the same therapist) accelerates and deepens the work quite considerably: the group allows for experimentation of many situations and stimulates more readily the emotions; individual work often helps each person refine his understanding and assimilate the experience gained, at his own pace.

You may either *begin* by individual interviews then rejoin a group at a later point, or inversely, begin by a group, *then* follow with individual sessions—as far as you may, of course, be content with one or the other formulas. Certain therapists follow only one procedure, but most offer both. You may also work individually with one therapist and participate in a group with another or other therapist/s—but that would involve some precautions to avoid a scattering of focus and certain patterns of avoidance.

How to find a serious therapist?
What precautions to use?
What guarantees to obtain?

This is a *crucial* question because the choice of a good therapist is more important than that of a good method!

It is important to *find out* if he was trained through a recognized institute, if he finished his course of studies and received a certificate or diploma, if he is supervised (that is controlled by a competent specialist). The simplest way is to *ask him directly*: if he hesitates to answer, for whatever reason, be careful! In fact, a good therapist who has been well prepared should be proud of his School and have nothing to hide.

If there is any doubt, don't hesitate to phone directly to the Institution where the therapist was trained. Currently, the title "psychotherapist" is not yet protected by law in all countries and in this case, anyone who so wishes may give himself this title, without any risk of legal problems. Therefore, you may find a certain number of poorly trained charlatans or gurus of different sects.

You may also request information from specialized organizations, as well as professional unions, associations or federations.

At any rate, it is preferable to meet with two or three therapists before making a definite choice for the many months of intimate and confidential work. It is important to feel at ease, in total security with the relationship. For certain therapists, the first interview is free.

First contacts? What to tell him?

It is not necessary to prepare in detail the first interview: it is better to stay spontaneous and improvise.

Usually, you will be asked to specify your intentions: what are you looking for? What difficulties are you experiencing? What results are you hoping for?

You may want to talk about other experiences with psychotherapy or whether you are currently taking any medication. It is generally discouraged to follow two *individual* psychotherapies at the same time (for example, an analytic psychotherapy and a Gestalt psychotherapy). On the other hand, it is possible to be in psychoanalysis and to simultaneously undertake a Gestalt *group* therapy, but such a combination would require the agreement of both psychotherapists.

Of course, everything that is said within a session is strictly covered by the rule of *professional secret*. If you send your own child to follow a therapy, the practitioner will be very discreet about what was said in the session and will give you only very general information; he will, however, listen to you with great attention.

Is my age an obstacle?

No! You may begin a Gestalt therapy at any age: certain therapists are more used to working with *young children* or with *adolescents*. One may also begin a therapy at an advanced age: such as, many clients consult therapists to deal with their difficulties at the time of retirement.

Of course, the style of therapy will be different according to the age of the client (as well as his cultural level and his personality). It may be more based on a verbal exchange or, on the other hand, emphasize other modes of expression—painting, games, movement, physical contact, etc.

How long does a therapy last?

This is very difficult to define in advance: everything depends on your problems, your personality, your objectives . . . as well as the preferred procedures of your psychotherapist! On the average, an individual therapy in depth will last one to several years, with a one-hour session per week, for about 40 hours per year (given time off for vacations, absences, sickness, etc.)—in all, a good hundred hours.

But certain therapies may be more rapid and just as effective (we sometimes notice very important and lasting changes after six months); others, on the contrary, may only begin to show some obvious effects after many months.

The association of a *group* therapy generally accelerates the process to a large extent, since the group more easily allows for physical and emotional movement—which influences the profound areas of the brain. Group therapy often involves work with co-therapists, of both genders, which can enhance both understanding as well as interactions.

There is also the possibility of a shorter, less profound therapy, for example, to deal with a difficult passage (death, separation, unemployment, etc.). In certain situations, several interviews (or even one intensive workshop of two or three days) may be enough to begin a positive process.

What are the risks?
The counter-indications?

The principle risk stems from an error in the choice of a "therapist": see the section above. Charlatans, without sufficient training, are not rare and certain sects (Scientology or Dianetics, for example) exploit various techniques from psychotherapy in order to create a dependency and not to encourage autonomy!

A well-conducted therapy with a competent therapist presents no risk at all: at most, there may be a certain imbalance in the relationship of the client with their partner, husband or wife, and this may cause a feeling of disorientation. And yet, if some real problems appear, it's generally because they were already brewing in the background and the therapy only served to *accelerate* a process of separation of the couple. However, most couples find their relationships reinforced and deepened as a result of a therapy: the positive results greatly outweigh the problems that may arise . . . Yet we hear most often of the problems, because they are more dramatic! When one partner of a couple begins a therapy, it may be a good idea in certain cases for the other one to undertake a process of personal discovery at the same time—but, preferably, with a different therapist, in order to avoid any interference: or, they may wish to begin a therapy together as a couple.

Can I help my child? My partner?

Naturally, you can ask for a therapy for your child, but this requires his explicit *agreement*, otherwise it will be quite ineffective. The therapist will generally see him *alone*, even if you accompany him for the visit. It is essential that he be able to express himself in full freedom, away from the presence of adults, including their parents. Be reassured, however, that therapists are accustomed to hear the many fantasies of children and don't take as hard facts all that they say (especially the therapists who specialize in working with children!). Progress may not be immediate: there may even be a period of increased agitation regarding certain problems, linked to the fact that the child feels "important": similar to what happens when a wound is opened to be healed, or when one goes to the dentist! Therefore, it is important to be patient . . . .

If your partner, husband or wife, wishes (or accepts) to begin a therapy, it is important that they make the appointment *themselves* and this not be done by you. It's a good idea to offer *several addresses* of different therapists, in order to allow him or her to feel that the *choice* is their own personal responsibility. A psychotherapist who is imposed upon someone is rarely effective.

We would like to work on our relationship as a couple.

Several formulas are possible:

- Each person may undertake an *individual* therapy on his/her own, with two *different* therapists.
- The two partners consult a therapist, or two therapists working *together*. In this case, the most usual, certain therapists will offer several individual sessions with each of the partners, in order to allow them to express any points that they may prefer not to bring up in front of their partner. These confidences are naturally respected in full respect of the "professional secret".
- The two partners take *an intensive workshop* of several days *together*, a type of "retreat" to discuss and evaluate their relationship.
- The two partners participate in a *workshop for couples only*. They work together in a group situation, with their "secrets shared" by a few others. Certain couples come to resolve their difficulties, even "succeed" to separate with minimal damage. Others come to support and nourish a relationship that is already satisfying. The mixture of these different situations is often very enriching and opens unexpected perspectives.

We have problems in our organization, in our company.

In this case, it is not a question of "therapy" but rather a *"psychosocial consultation"*. The problems or concerns may be of all types: conflicts or institutional crisis; change in management or restructuring; encouragement of creativity, etc. (See chapter about *Socio-Gestalt*).

The consultant should be *specialized in this type of work* which involves particular precautions to avoid unnecessary turmoil. It is recommended to have the tacit agreement of both the management as well as representatives of the personnel. The work could be very specific (lasting one or two days only) or take place more on a regular basis, covering a longer time period (such as, one or several days per month or per quarter).

TRAINING

I would like to become a professional practitioner in Gestalt Therapy: what should I do?

The *conditions for admission for the training program (or pre-requisites)* are somewhat variable depending on the organizations or schools as well as the country. For Europe, standards have been established by the EAGT *(European Association for Gestalt Therapy* <www.eagt. org>*)* and by the *EAP (European Association for Psychotherapy* <www. europsyche.org>*)*.

To give you an idea, here are the conditions for admission for practitioners in Gestalt (in the fields of psychotherapy, psychosocial work, or within organizations) at *l'Ecole Parisienne de Gestalt* (Paris School of Gestalt) in France:

- a certain personal *maturity* (the average age of students is around 40 years, and candidates of less than 30 are the exception;
- an in-depth experience of *personal therapy* (individual or in group, and preferably, both);
- a cultural level of "bac+3", either: a "licence" (French Bachelor Degree after about 3 years in a University) in Psychology or Educational Sciences; a professsional diploma in a medical or psychosocial profession such as Special Education, Social Service, Nursing, Paramedical professions, Psychology, Medicine, Teaching, Adult Education, Organizational Consulting, Human Resources Development, etc. Certain waivers may be accorded;
- a certain *practice of the original profession* (for example, at least two years);
- an entrance examination at the school or institution chosen: in the form of interviews, selection workshops and a probationary year.

The requirements include a balanced personality, flexibility and openness to others, dynamism and creativity, and a capacity for personal implication, both profound and controlled.

The basic training lasts 4 years, on a part-time basis: in the form of periodic meetings (for example, 5 sessions of 4 or 5 days per year) or intensive sessions (for example, three weeks in summer, for two successive years—after a probationary year.)

The program includes *theoretical and methodological* courses in Psychotherapy and Psychopathology, the acquisition of a certain number of *techniques, practical* experimentation, *supervised* practice, case studies, etc., as well as the preparation and presentation of a *thesis* at the end of the curriculum. This process is followed in an attitude of ongoing personal commitment.

The basic training may be followed by an *advanced training* during *two or more* years, including a regular *supervision,* courses to deepen and broaden understanding (Psychopathology, Transference, etc.) and leading to a certificate or *Diploma of Gestalt Therapy.*

The total training lasts a minimum of 2000 hours, including a personal psychotherapy, theory and methodology, 2 years of supervised practice, 150 hours of supervision, psychopathology, etc.

The *European Certificate of Psychotherapy* (ECP) involves a total of 7 years of theoretical and practical studies (3,200 hours).

To give an idea, to-day, in France, there are *about one thousand certified practitioners in Gestalt Therapy.* The majority work independently in a private practice and receive clients in *individual* sessions. Certain also offer therapy in *groups.* Others are specialized for certain categories of clients (children or adolescents, couples, sexology, mentally disturbed, bulimics, etc.). Some are trainers or consultants in organizations. At the present time, there is no unemployment in this profession, in France! . . . A specific law with a set of official regulations and procedures is now being prepared.

INDEX

FOR FURTHER INFORMATION

For more information, you can contact directly the author:

Serge GINGER
Clinical psychologist and psychotherapist
Founder of the EPG:
École Parisienne de Gestalt (Paris School of Gestalt)

President of FORGE:
Fédération internationale des Organismes de Formation à la Gestalt (International Federation of Gestalt Training Organizations)

Secretary general of the FF2P:
Fédération Française de Psychothérapie et Psychanalyse (French National Umbrella for Psychotherapy and Psychoanalysis)

Registrar of the EAP (European Association for Psychotherapy), Chair of the TAC (Training Accreditation Committee).
183 rue Lecourbe.
75015 PARIS (FRANCE) Tél.: + 331 5368 6458
Fax: + 331 5368 6457
GSM: + 336 0976 2651
E-mail: ginger@noos.fr
or:
EPG: École Parisienne de Gestalt 27 rue Froidevaux.
75014 PARIS (FRANCE)
Tél.: + 33 1 43 22 40 41
Fax: + 33 1 43 22 50 53
E-mail: epg@gestalt.asso.fr
Web-site: www.gestalt.asso.fr
AVAILABLE
GINGER S. & al. (1995). *International Glossary of Gestalt Therapy terms.*
edited by FORGE, Paris (*176 pages*).
Price: 20 US $ or 20 uro.
One hundred specific Gestalt terms and expressions, explained and translated in 8 languages, with definitions:Dutch, English, French, German, Italian, Portuguese, Russian, Spanish.